Rick Magers

# UNINVITED

## ~ To the Everglades ~

~ o ~

A nightmare of pythons

A novel

by

Rick Magers

Published in the United States of America

by Americans

@

# GBP

## Grizzly Bookz Publishing

A Not-For-Profit Organization

Rick Magers

Printed in the United States

by

Americans

@

Snowfall Press

OR

CreateSpace

All proceeds from the sale of books
authored by Rick Magers are
donated to the
following.

100 years old Smallwood Store in Chokoloskee Florida.
Katia Solomon, the girl in Ladybug and the Dragon.
The Gentle Barn-Animal Haven, Santa Clarita, California.
Elephant Sanctuary in Hohenwald, Tennessee.
Homeless animal caregivers wherever we find them.
People and animals needing help we meet along the way.
Down and outers who need a meal or a bottle of MD 20/20

# Books by this author: 2017

Dark Caribbean

The McKannahs

The McKannahs ~ together again ~

Ladybug and the Dragon

The Black Widowmaker/Satan's Dark Angels

Uninvited

America

Carib Indian

The Face Painter

80 Short Stories

A Sacred Vow

It's A Dog's Life

The Ghosts of Chokoloskee

CALUSA ~warriors from a distant past~

2084 ~a world in peril~

Pioneers of South Florida

Coming in winter 2017—2099 ~a world in repair~

All books by this author are available at:

Amazon.com

or

contact him at **magersrick@yahoo.com**

A signed copy will be shipped to you.

A description of each book is on the last page.

## PREFACE

The original idea for this book about the pythons that are moving into the Everglades, devouring all wildlife, and then taking over, probably began smoldering between my big, floppy, freckled red ears, when I was a teenager growing up on the Miami River and later in Hialeah, a suburb of Miami Florida.

Three adventurous friends and I regularly prepared for an expedition into the nearby Everglades. We loaded the BB guns chock-full of BBs, and carried a couple of spare tubes in our Levi's. It was a precaution, in case we ran into a wild boar, black bear, panther, crocodile or an alligator that had walked across U S Highway 27 and into the wet marshlands, and then decided to stay. Luck was on their side. We never ran into any of them—we did however come across the track of something much more frightening.

With a couple of cucumbers for lunch that I had shoved into the pockets of my Levis, I stepped out of the 1933 Willis sedan that my dad gave me when I was thirteen. Surveying the savannah stretching towards the horizon, I levered my deadly Red Ryder. The BB hit the fence post and buried into the rain-softened old cypress. I was ready.

A long hot hour of walking through wet grass had brought us halfway to a very big hammock. All four of us had previously seen it in the distance, but had never investigated. Being the expedition leader, I raised my arm, stopping all forward progress. I had stumbled upon something so chilling that I have never forgotten.

Coming at us from our left was the swerving; eight-inch deep and twelve-inch wide track of what we all later agreed could only be one creature.

One of only two Hialeah kids that I knew came from wealthy families, (we knew they were wealthy because both of their fathers brought the dorky kids to Hialeah Elementary and Jr. High, every morning in a shiny new car) that attended our school, had told us earlier about a huge 'pet' python that he turned loose in the Everglades. "It got too big," he said, "so daddy drove us to Flamingo State Park so we could release it out of the cage that was already too small." I have since wondered if his mother or grandmother was the person who brought that first hyacinth into Florida, the unsuccessful eradication of which has cost millions of taxpayer dollars.

Cautiously we walked toward the hammock right along that swerving path 'it' had made. We looked for signs of feet out at the side, which a gator would make as it walked—there were none. "We're walking," my friend, Don Miller said, "in the fairly fresh track that only a big python could have made. Looking down at this track, that sucker's probably as long as that bigass boat you live on, Mage."

That bigass boat was a 73' wooden Coast Guard Cutter that my dad converted to a houseboat. Thinking about a snake that long caused me to stop. I was in the lead, so once again they all stopped.

After I had eaten only one of my salted cucumbers, we agreed unanimously to turn around and head back.

~ O ~

*I* never forgot that eight-inch deep, one-foot wide track that we had been walking in, back in the early 50s.

**FOREWORD**

This book is a fact-based account of what I feel certain will become, in the not so distant future, the heralding in of the demise of a one-of-a-kind piece of extraordinary landscape.

~ The Florida Everglades ~

Rick Magers

Many people that I talked to while researching, were astounded to learn for the first time, that there is no place on Planet Earth that even remotely resembles The Everglades of South Florida.

Imagine a wildlife sanctuary where 20,000 pound, 14′ high, woolly mammoths once roamed, and small horses weighing only 75 pounds, the mesohippus, once ran alongside his big brother, the 500-pound hipparion. Imagine giant ground sloths that stood 15′ high on their back legs.

With all of these images in mind, it should be obvious that modern humankind made a grave error by constructing a land-based highway, once known as Alligator Alley, to link Ft. Lauderdale with Naples. A road raised on pilings, as was done across the bayous of Louisiana, would have allowed traffic to commute back and forth while the River of Grass continued its slow progress across the aquifers that bring life to South Florida—as potable fresh water.

That blunder, combined with ignoring the fact that an uninvited species of snake, the python, has been dining on the Everglades birds, bird eggs, and animals for over forty years—since the days when pythons were sold as pets—might very well be the ringing of the Everglades death knell.

I recommend that you visit the Everglades soon, if you can bear attending the wake of a once incredibly unique piece of our

American heritage—it will be like watching huge bulldozers backfilling the Grand Canyon to build a trailer park on top.

Going into the Everglades without a guide might become a source of lifetime nightmares.

*~ If you live to have them ~*

**O**ne last look around, and then Charlie listened for noise that did not belong…Charlie Potter slowly lifted his head up above the mound he had just come to…His eyes were not ready for what he saw.

~ **O** ~

"Oh, no! Oh my God, oh!" Charlie thrashed around, arms flailing as though he was a Chokoloskee chicken about to take flight.

"Charlie, wake up, wake up, goddammit." Lily-Mae, his live-in girlfriend and childhood sweetheart since their days growing up in Ochopee, tried to hold his legs down as she yelled.

Rick Magers

Charlie's arm hit her forehead and knocked her to the floor, but the motion caused him to fall off the narrow bed too.

Charlie slowly stood and looked around the moonlit room. He refused to sleep in a dark room, so he could see her struggling to get on her feet in the faint glow of the quarter moon and the nightlight in the wall beside the bed. "What in the hell are you doing down there on that floor, Lily-Mae?"

"You knocked me off the goddamn bed again, y'crazy bastard."

"Aw shit! I musta been dreamin' about that big snake again."

"That ain't dreaming, Charlie. Nightmares like that one you been having, can blow a hole in your heart n' send to the graveyard."

# BEGIN

**F**ourteen year-old Jeremy slipped quietly out the back door of his father's hunting cabin.

After two years of heated arguing, his mother had given in and allowed him to board a plane in New Jersey and spend part of the summer with his father in Naples, Florida.

The ride in his father's airboat filled the boy's mind with re-runs of Wild Kingdom. "We're gonna spend the whole week out in the Everglades?"

"Yep," his father answered, "bout time you see the real side of life—a real man's world." His father's smile thrilled the short, pale, eighty-pound young boy.

The first day at the small cabin, Emmitt brought out a new Remington .22 rifle and handed it to Jeremy. "I think it's time you have your own rifle, son."

Jeremy stood transfixed with his mouth hanging open and his eyes stretched wide as he held a gun for the very first time in his life.

"It's not loaded, but don't ever point it at anything anyway, because so-called unloaded guns have killed lots of amateurs. "I'm gonna teach you how to clean it, load it, shoot it, and every one of the can-do and no-can-do rules."

A quart bottle of Jack Daniels sat on the table next to a small Igloo of ice cubes. Emmitt filled his glass. After a long sip, he opened the fresh box of ammunition and put his heart into teaching his son how to load, shoot, and care for his first gun—between sips of JD.

By the time the sun was approaching the tops of the western trees, Jeremy had filled several targets with holes and was feeling more confidence than at any other point in his short life.

Rick Magers

Standing less than four feet tall, Jeremy had become a devout mama's boy, and the bait for every bully in the school. His mother had divorced Emmitt when Jeremy was five, and then moved back to New Jersey to be near her parents. Between them and Jeremy's over-protective mother, the young, too small, boy had been sheltered from everything that makes a boy a boy. He had never been exposed to the basic essentials that prepare a boy for eventual manhood.

The second day of firearm instruction began at noon when his father took a short pull from the second bottle of Jack Daniels. After he swished it around in his mouth, he swallowed and let the warmth flow through his body. "Ahhhhhhhh," he crooned as he swung his short legs out from beneath the mosquito netting. After revolving his head several times, he shook off the JD cobwebs, and lifted the net, and shoved it behind so he could stand.

After scooping two strawberry yogurts into his still cotton-lined maw, he looked at his son; a carbon copy of his father, albeit slightly smaller. Jeremy was sitting on the wide windowsill with both his feet hanging outside. "Didja have some breakfast, son?"

"Yessir," he turned and smiled at his father, "I fixed myself a big bowl of Special-K."

"That's good, son, y'gotta start each day with a full belly." Emmitt walked to the nearest window and looked at the sky, and then scanned the hammock he had built the cabin in. "We'll go out later this afternoon and see if we can shoot a coupla Chokoloskee chickens for dinner."

"What are chuckleiskee chickens?"

"Curlew," Emmitt answered, "actually they're ibis, a local native bird that's a lot better eatin than them store-bought, force-fed buzzards them stores're sellin as real chickens." He grinned at his son who grinned back, even though the boy had no idea what his dad was talking about.

The only food Jeremy had ever seen except restaurant food was either packaged, frozen, or in a can.

Afternoon came, and then went out with the second empty whiskey bottle. Jeremy listened to Emmitt ramble on about his hard times, with no used cars selling—fuel to go out in his airboat being so high he couldn't use it very often—what a bitch Jeremy's mother was—how she'd ruined his life, etc., etc. After a few more mumbled complaints, he started at the beginning again.

That is when Jeremy said he was too tired and went into his bedroom. He sat staring into the dark hammock, dreaming of alligators, panthers, bobcats, and all the other animals that his father had filled his dreams with each time during the past year when the boy called him.

Jeremy suffered through another day of waiting for his father to get up and take him into the swamp. When Emmitt drank himself into a stupor and fell asleep in the old recliner, Jeremy went to his room and began putting together the things he would need to go hunting when the sun came up.

The following morning Jeremy waited until he was far away from the cabin and deep into the dense hammock before he sat down in a clearing and got out a peanut butter and jelly sandwich. After wadding the paper bag and shoving it beneath a fallen tree trunk, he washed down the last of the sandwich with a cold Pepsi. He then pulled out the box of .22 caliber shells to fill his very own Remington pump-action rifle.

With the tube full of bullets, he pumped one into the chamber, exactly as his father had taught him. Jeremy then checked to be certain that the safety was on, just as he was told to do—between Jack Daniels breaks.

Three hundred yards from the cabin, Jeremy had slowly made his way through the hammock toward the sun-bathed area ahead that he had been using as a guide.

*Boy oh boy*, he thought as he stalked silently through a wild jungle of huge cypress trees, palmetto, and natural scrub brush, *dad will sure be surprised if I come back with a couple of chikiliskee chickens, or a rabbit, or som'n else to eat tonight.*

He heard only a slight noise prior to the beast rushing out to grab him. The new rifle was knocked out of his hand. His mouth was open to yell when his face was pushed into the swampy marsh he had been walking on.

Faster than a lightning bolt, the beast threw a loop over his upper body, and then added a second loop. Once his catch was lifted by the incredible strength of a muscular body so powerful that it could lift and crush an animal five times its weight, a third loop was thrown on top of the other two.

A group of rescuers could not have saved Jeremy by this time. The three loops, each about eight inches in diameter, had constricted so thoroughly that everything from his waist up had been crushed so completely, that all air trapped in the boy's lungs had been squeezed out.

A fourth loop was added around the head and the constriction began tightening. Only a few minutes after the nineteen-foot-long reticulated python struck Jeremy's upper torso, it was being completely pulverized into a malleable mush that could easily be swallowed.

Less than an hour later, only the legs remained outside the huge snake's jaws. With each constriction, the cadaver went farther into the snake. The size six artificial leather boots did not slow the process down a bit.

Three hours after the python spotted his meal, it was moving slowly toward the wet marshlands surrounding the hammock. It was where this same beast had often found an unsuspecting deer drinking, or a five or six-foot -long alligator that didn't know that it was making a fatal error by inspecting the snake as a possible meal.


2017

~ Pythons are the new rulers of the Everglades ~


It was the 4th of July weekend when I first arrived in Everglades City. 2019 had been a hot summer in Miami, but the heat in that small town beat anything I had ever seen. Even the dogs weren't up and walking around like they did when I was in this area working on a story for my editor back in 2016, and that was a really hot summer too. But nothing like this. Weather forcasters said that 2020 was going to break records that had been around for over a century, and it was beginning to look like they were right.

Yan Shen was the editor/owner/publisher of a new magazine that he had creatid, with my help, from scratch a short time before we both graduated from Miami Uni in 2015. Yan's magazine, A BRAND NEW FLORIDA, took off like a scalded-ass orang-u-tan, just as the inheritance he got from his grandma ran out. Yan had started that year in about September with a very small personal hygiene bag; underwear, two pairs of pants, a pair of old worn thin sneakers, and about a dozen t-shirts that he regularly replaced at Jorge Meyer Exposito's Used Clothing Store a block or so from our

Rick Magers

building.

I say *our* building, not because I invested money into Yan's dream, but since I was his only writer back at the start, I figured we were in it together.

Yan hired me just before I graduated from Miami-U at the same time he did. Six months before graduation he inherited a hundred grand from his grandmother in Ohio. She moved back to Ohio after her husband died in 1990, and after that she lived quite well until early 2000.

Yan was her only grandson and she sent a letter every week to let him know she was doing fine. That was until she had a heart attack at 99 and fell out of her chair while dining. Shirley Shen was dead before she hit the floor of the restaurant.

Yan was always very good to me, partially I suppose because of my wealthy bluenose Boston family, who sent me five grand each month while I was in college. They advised me to continue until I had my Masters degree in journalism, and then go on for a doctorate in another field – 'any goddamn field' – I was told my grandfather roared, 'just so Engeburt stays in college far from Boston.'

That is not what was said in a letter, but that's what I was told by my Uncle Conrad. I never met another relative on my father's side of the family that I thought was worth a two-dollar shit at the train depot's filthy money-potti.

Rick Magers

During my high school years in Boston, Mass, my regular weekend junkets to Martha's Vineyard and Nantucket had become fodder for my growing legend. My stuffy father, a bank owner, or I should say, banks owner—he had thirty when I left home for college—once summed up his attitude about me to my prim and proper mother. Intently listening through the small floor register in my upstairs bedroom, I heard it all. "Engeburt has probably sired a tribe of bastards, no doubt totaling hundreds, and due to the powerful genes of our many unsoiled and pure generations of the Fetterman Family, they will all probably be and look just like him."

I'm quite certain that he graphically exaggerated the amount of children left behind in my wake. My libido was, however, one of vast and inexhaustible demands. That, and considering the fact that I refused to use those damn rubbers, except to make a hillariously sugestive balloon during class, perhaps dear old dad didn't hit far off the correct number after all.

In May of this year, 2020, Yan approached holding a copy of the Miami Herald, folded to a specific article. He softly said, "Here Eng, read this."

I took the paper and read the article as Yan sipped his ever-present coffee. "Damn," I blurted out as I read, "a thirteen and a half foot long reticulated Burmese python has apparently crushed and devoured a four-year-old Seninole girl right in her own village." Yan reached for the paper as his head tilted back to drain the cup.

"It goes on," he said while rolling the Herald back up, "to state that the Miccosukee tribe is aggressively urging those assholes at the Everglades National Park Service to increase the bounty on those snakes from the current two hundred bucks to at least a thousand or more." Yan looked up, "Engeburt, dear ole pal, I think it is about the right time for you to follow United States Representative Horace Greeley's suggestion."

I pinched my lips and raised my eyebrows, "I'd much rather go south into the Caribbean and see if I can change my luck."

~ O ~

A bit after dawn on July 3rd I had slithered down into my new 2020 Ford Thunder Eagle tudor coupe and headed west, as ole Horace Greeley and my boss had suggested. By 10:00 AM, with a coffee stop, and later, a breakfast stop at a Miccosukee restaurant on Tamiami Trail, I was close to Highway 29, where I would then turn south to go into Everglades City.

I slowed down to 70 because ahead, I could see a pickup truck pulled off the road and almost touching the steel guard next to the canal. A quick check in the rear mirror and I saw nothing was coming, so I pulled in behind the truck.

I could see steam rushing out, and a tall guy standing back a bit, shaking his head. When he spotted me he just sorta nodded and gave a small wave.

Glancing into the rear view mirror again I saw there was still nothing coming our way, so I climbed out and approached the guy. "Radiator?" I asked when I was near him.

"Nah, just a dern hose, but it's a sorry time for it, be cause ahm s'pose to meet a guy in," he looked at his watch, "about fifteen minutes."

"Where y'gotta meet him?"

"City Hall in Everglades."

"That's where I'm heading, so hop in my car if you think your truck'll be okay until we get back here with a hose, or whatever you'll need to get her running again."

"I'll sure take y'up on that, pal, cause this guy's big in state g'ment."

He left the hood up and hopped in. We breezed right through the small town of Ochopee, and a short run later he said, "Go easy now and turn left at the flasher 'cause the Sheriff Sub-Station's right there on the left."

I didn't bother telling him that I'd been here before. Five minutes after turning south we were pulling into City Hall.

"Thanks pal," he said climbing out.

I nodded toward the Marathon mini-mart we'd just passed, "I'll get myself a cup of coffee and wait out here for you, so we can get whatever y'need n' go getcher truck running."

He stopped and looked at me, "Y'ain't from 'roun here pal, butcher damn sure no Yankee. Ah preciate it, man. See you in a while."

~ O ~

I got my very first hint at what the python thing was all about while I stood outside of the Kangaroo Mini-Mart sipping my hot cup of coffee.

"Goddammit, Mort, I juss now tole ya why them dern g'mint assholes ain't gonna raise the bounty on 'em there snakes."

"Yeah Relapse," Morton Gomez said, "but yer always saying them guys ain't gonna let that money get away from 'em, and it wasn't but a while back they jacked it up to six hunert fer four footers n' up, an five hunert fer under four footers."

Relapse Watson just shook his head slowly and kept sipping his breakfast. "I still say we ain't never gonna see eleven, or even a thousand, fer any over four feet."

"You thought we'd never get paid for juss the head, but that's all them fellers gotta bring in now." Morton dropped his foot from the wall next to the bagged-ice holding box and put both hands over his head and stretched before putting the other foot against a wall and leaning back.

Rick Magers

"Thet was all Abner's doin," Relapse almost shouted, "an them sonuvabitches are still squawkin about it." His green, hairy-tooth smile caused Morton to lean back, even though his teeth were exactly like them. "Havin the guv'nah as a friend is a good deal, cause that means they cain't do shit about it."

"I don't reckon they're really friends," Morton said as he leaned farther back, "he just hires Ab to carry him out now n' then to catch a snook."

"Goddammit Mort, the man comes t'Abs barbies an even had a famous country band come n' play at Jungle Jew's last birthday party. Y'reckon juss a damn ole fishin customer's gonna do thet?"

Morton Gomez just shook his head, "If Ab's got hisself some rich folks like the gov for friends, then how come he lives in that damn swamp buggy mosta the time?"

"At's cause he likes livin out in 'em Everglades." Relapse lifted his can of breakfast and emptied it, "He ain't never took t'folks like his uncle, Jungle Jew, does. An besides, that's where Ab's always made his livin."

Morton took the last sip from his can of Budweiser then tossed it into the weeds beside the store. "I reckon if I had rich friends like thet, I'd be livin in one o' them nice places alongside the Barron River in Everglades."

Relapse Watson shook his head, "Ahm goin over n' see if Delvin needs any help cleanin traps." He headed toward his rusty old bicycle that was leaning against the wall around the corner. "I'll see ya later, Mort."

"Less have us another can of breakfast, Relapse. That damn brother of yours ain't gonna give you enough t'pay for the rubber you're gonna wear off them tires goin over there."

"Mebbe so, Mort, but if I stay roun you much longer, sure's hell I'm gonna ketch what you got."

"Catch what I got, what the hell's that?"

"Ignernce." Relapse yelled over his shoulder as he peddled away toward the Barron River.

As I walked back toward City Hall, I just sipped my coffee and thought about what I just heard. *Six hundred bucks for four footers and up, and five hundred for under four footers. Those damn pythons are gonna make some of these swamp boys rich.*

Just as I took the last sip, the guy I brought here came out and walked toward me. "Took a little longer than I thought. Thanks for waitin." He held out his hand, "I'm Abner Brown."

"Engelburt Fetterman...Burt with a u, but Eng to my friends." I took his hand and shook it—it was kinda like shaking hands with a professional arm-wrestler...like leather wrapped around some bundled steel cable.

"Everyone around here calls me Ab." His eyebrows scrunched down, "Burt with a u, huh?" Abner paused a moment before asking, "How about Burt instead of Eng? Any local folks you meet around here's gonna ask if you're Chinese."

"Wouldn't be the first time." Engelburt grinned, "I was Burt at school up to fifth grade. Mom heard someone call me Burt and about had a meltdown right there in the principal's office, so I was Engelburt at the new school she transferred me to that same day."

"What was you in the principal's office for?"

"Punching the shit out of a big bully that slapped my skinny little Haitian pal."

Abner just grinned. "C'mon, Burt, let's go over to Win-Car hardware n' see if Jim has the right hose."

"Sure, let's go," I said and climbed into my Thunder Eagle.

"Nice car," Ab commented as we pulled out, "what the hell is it?"

"She's this year's brand new version of Ford Motor Company's electric Thunder Eagle. My boss and also best friend inherited a shot in the arm last month and bought it for me." I turned and grinned, "To make up I guess, for me writing his new magazine's best columns for a solid year of Ramen Noodle breakfasts, lunches, and dinners."

"I thought it must a new kind of muffler, but it's electric, huh?"

"Yep, and they're good for two hundred miles at full power, and then when the warning lights up, y'got fifty miles at half power to find a recharge station, or a place with two hundred and twenty volts where you can plug your own charger in."

Rick Magers

"Holy shit," Abner said as he took a greater interest, and scanned the gauges. He leaned over to get a better look at the odometer. "A hundred and twenty, ha. That's probably like the two hundred MPH the Japs put on their motorcycle speedometers before sending them here."

"Nossir!" I glanced over at Abner, "I had her pegged out up on Alligator Alley right after I got it. I was heading toward Fort Myers Beach, and could see there was nobody else on the road so early, so I opened her up. Took less than two minutes to peg out." I glanced at him again, "Great technology, huh?"

"Damn sure is. I read a while back that they were on the right track, but figured it'd be a while before they'd have one like this on the market." Abner turned and looked at the small rear compartment, "Ford finally went back to a two-seater again, huh?"

"Yep, one pal or one gal."

"Ha ha!" Abner laughed, "That is exactly how I have it. I do not carry but one other person in my swamp castle."

"What's that?" I asked.

"M'swamp buggy. I'll take you along next time out, if y'want."

"Just gimme a holler, n' I'll be ready in a minute."

"Will do." Abner looked around the inside again. "If I get a good batch o' snakes, I reckon I'll hafta go have a look at one o' these."

After getting his truck running, Abner Brown invited me to go have lunch with him. "Meet me," he said, "over at The Seafood Junction at eleven-thirty and lunch's on me."

"Sounds good t'me," I answered, "that's the place you pointed out just down the road from the hardware?"

"Yep, friend o' mine named Billy Potter, reopened the old Captain's Table Restaurant a few years ago. Darn good food and he has a nice inside lounge and a screened in bar outside." Abner's smile widened, "Plus good lookin waitresses."

I waited until he pulled out, to be sure his truck was running okay, then followed him west on Tamiami Trail toward State Road 29 at Carnestown. A few minutes later we turned south and headed back toward Everglades City.

A little before eleven-thirty, I saw that he had just pulled into the restaurant parking lot, so I parked beside his truck in the huge parking lot that surrounded the restaurant. Abner got out and we headed inside.

"You said the guy who opened this was once a stone crab trapper?"

"Yeah," Abner answered, "for quite a few years, and he was one of the big operations. Had lotsa traps and a good boat, but decided to sell out and open a restaurant."

"This one?"

"Nah, several years before he opened this one, he had a new

one built on the causeway going to Chokoloskee. You'll see it on the left when you head over there. It's a big ole place on the left near the observation tower. He named it The Oyster House."

"He still own that one too?"

"Nope, sold it." He turned and grinned, "Probably was thinking about retiring, and along came some guy that offered him more money than he could turn down.

Wasn't so long though before he was here remodeling the old Captain's Table into this place."

I looked around, "Seems like he knew what he was doing."

"Yeah," Abner said, "everybody says Billy's as good a cook as he was a crabber, and he was a damn good one."

We both had a piece of Key Lime Pie, and when I went to lay down a ten dollar bill as a tip, Abner said, "Put it back in your pocket, Burt, I got it all." He smiled, "Y'don't get many opportunities to have a real free lunch, tip and all," he grinned, "just like y'ain't gonna see many strangers stop along the highway to offer you a helping hand, these days."

We'd had one of the best lunches I'd enjoyed in a long time. I loved those home made potato chips that the waitress brought us to munch on while we waited.

Abner stopped beside his truck. "Burt," he said, "have a look around town and over on Chokoloskee, too, but don't check into a place. I'll ask around and find you a good place to stay. Y'said

Rick Magers

you're gonna be here about a month, so lemme find you a place that'll be nice but not cost you an arm and leg. And also you won't hafta worry about that nice car o' yours when you're out in the Glades with me." He raised his arm to look at his watch, "Meet me in the outside chickee bar, right here at Billy's, at six o'clock this afternoon."

I instinctually knew that I had made a good friend by stopping to assist Abner Brown.


A little before six I was sitting in the chickee bar on the outside of the Seafood Junction. It's attached and has an entrance to the dining room, but it's just like being outside, minus the swamp angels and saber-toothed gnats.

I was chatting with the cute bartender, Maggie, when Abner walked in. "Hi, Burt, hello Maggie darlin, I think a Chokoloskee Cocktail oughta do it, but I'm gonna hafta drink it standing up."

I watched as she made the drink, because it was new to me. After tossing some ice in the glass, Maggie poured the ice-filled glass almost full of vodka then added what appeared to be fifteen or so drops of Coca Cola.

Standing it in front of Ab, who was still standing, she asked, "You get bit in the ass again by a gator?"

"Nope." Ab took a sip before answering, "Ain't got nothin to sit on, cause I worked my ass off all afternoon."

Maggie just grinned and walked toward a customer,

"I shoulda known better than to ask."

"Rough afternoon?" I asked.

"Nah, not really. When I wasn't driving back n' forth checking on things, I was sitting across the desk from one of those goddamn park rangers." After another sip, Ab turned around and leaned back against the bar. "I can't get those guys to understand how critical it is that a larger bounty be put on the pythons." He turned to me, "Burt, you won't believe how many are out there until you see it yourself. I know where there's a five-acre hammock that has at least a thousand of 'em and there's not another animal or bird anywhere near that place."

After a sip of his Chokoloskee Cocktail, Abner turned toward Engelburt, "Burt, I looked through my files last night to see if I could find an old newspaper article about those pythons. I did and it was written seven years ago in two thousand and thirteen for the Washington Post by Darryl Fears." As he was talking, Abner pulled out the folded article he had in his shirt pocket and handed it to Burt.

Abner sipped as Engelburt read, and then looked up, "Says here, Ab, that there might be a hundred thousand pythons in the Glades, and that most of the bobcats, opossums, raccoons, rabbits, and foxes too are gone." Burt shook his head and handed the article back to Abner.

Burt pulled out his small Sony recorder and then hit rewind. A moment later he played back what Ab had said earlier. "Do you mind if I record stuff like that? I'll let you read everything before I leave, and will edit out anything you don't want going into print."

"Sure, Burt, go ahead and record it all, because I want people to know why we're gonna lose the Everglades if some better policies aren't put into effect soon." He finished his drink and waved at Maggie to bring two more. "I'm not sure there's much hope no matter what they do. I reckon them dumbass desk monkeys up in Tallahassee have dragged their goddamn feet for too long already."

Abner whipped his arm up to look at his Timex, then blurted out, "Shit, I'm ten minutes late." He put his drink on the bar and looked at me, "I was supposed to call someone about getting you a house to live in for a month'r so. I'll go outside and use my cell phone."

A few minutes later, he was back, and climbed up on the stool beside me, "A friend of mine checked with his mom and says she has a house facing Chokoloskee Bay that'll be available for at least six weeks, mebbe more. Forty-five hundred and it's ready for you to move right in, plus it also includes housekeeping three times a week."

I grinned, "No Budget Motels around here, huh?"

"If there was," Ab said with a smile, "it would cost you three hundred and fifty a night now in the summer, and twice that during the season."

"I know, because I called trying to get a place in town, and only one had a room available. She sounded like a dot-head Indian that barely spoke English, but when she said two seexty fife each night, I understood her. Key West is like that now too during summer, and winter prices are only for the snowbuzzards, because they can afford it."

"Never been there," Ab said, "but a lotta people that come here say it's too damn crowded even during the hot months, and they ain't goin back down there."

"I spent a week there this past winter writing about all of the trap bouys that vacationing boaters complain about. It'll really hafta be som'n special to get me back down there."

"I wouldn't go there," Ab said with a grin, "if the beer and clapp shots were both free."

"Tell me how to find this place and I'll go pay her for the six weeks of rent. I'm wondering now if even that's gonna be enough time."

"Let's have one more," Ab said, "and you can follow me. After you drop your stuff, I'll take you for a ride in my airboat so you can see a little of what we're up against."

"What were you saying earlier about Alligator Alley being the first death blow to the Everglades?"

Rick Magers

"Well," Abner said, "it is now simply a dam that separates the northern section of the Everglades from the Southern. They put in some flow-throughs that're having the same effect that the python rodeo did that the politicians endorsed back in 2013. It's like putting a goddamn Mickey Mouse bandage over a twenty millimeter cannon wound. The medic knows you're gonna die but it makes him feel good doing something, and if you're a dumbass you think it might save you."

Ab paused to drink half of his Chokoloskee Cocktail. "There were some good engineers back in the fifties and sixties when they first began talking about building that damn highway across the Everglades from Lauderdale to Naples. They told the state to do what Lousiana did when they crossed their bayous, because if you build a traditional road, and then those Everglades will be dead in a hundred years."

Burt asked, "What did Lousiana do?"

"Built their roads up on pilings so the water could move like it always had."

"Alligator Alley was opened in nineteen sixty-nine wasn't it?"

"Yep," Abner said with a frown, "and the Glades're already half dead."

Engelburt shook his head slowly. "What a disaster it'll be if the only Everglades on the planet dies."

"Not for the land developers, and the politicians who will," Ab then wobbled his eyebrows as he picked up his drink, "for a fat fee, authorize all of the land between South Florida's east and west coast to be filled in for development."

"Damn," Burt groaned, "those high-rise condos and the gated communities coast-to-coast from Lake Okeechobee all the way to Tamiami Trail."

"And Disneyworld South," Ab said, "with easy access right off the Trail, which will be a six lane highway. And there'll be another fifty golf courses and a dozen Country Clubs." He wobbled his black eyebrows up and down again, "A Snowbuzzard's dream come true."

~ O ~

Chokoloskee was not the barren chunk of swamp land that I was expecting. Until the 1950s it was the largest island in the well known chain of Ten Thousand Islands. A three mile causeway was pumped in, and an asphalt road was laid over the shell base, making it easily accessable to local fishermen and tourists. Within half a century, the quiet little fishing village, only a short drive east of Naples, was no more. Laws were enacted that made commercial fishing a local livelihood of the past. Young people raised there now had to become part of the local tourist-entertainment-entourage, or move away from the home area they loved.

I sure wasn't expecting to see two huge motorhome parks at the end of the causeway, but there they were, and later I found another big camping park on the west side of the island. I passed a few very nice homes and a gated resort as we continued south, but when I saw the several acre estate on the left, just before we entered what Ab called Viking Country, I began to see the appeal of this little-known paradise at the end of highway 29.

Before we turned into Viking Country, there was a five or six acre estate with a mansion sitting behind a half-mile or so of chainlink fence. It was a beautiful mansion that would not be out of place in Beverly Hills or Monterey, California's famous Seven Mile Drive.

I stopped my Ford Thunder Eagle to enjoy a brief momentary daydream as Ab walked back and leaned down, "That's a very good reason for guys like us to buy a Lotto ticket every Wednesday and Saturday."

"Got mine in the glove compartment. Is this place," I made a nod toward the mansion, "the president's winter getaway shack, or a vacation place for the Chinese boss, now that they own America?"

"Neither," Ab grinned, "belongs to a guy that could buy China. Made trillions making coffin nails."

"Lucky Strikes or Camels?"

"Phillip Morris."

"Well I'll be damn."

I sat there shaking my head. "And I thought my dad is a rich old fart, but his few million would be walking-around pocket money for this guy."

Ab had been looking over the top of my car, and bent down, "I've often wondered just how many in his family have died of lung cancer."

"Yessir," I chuckled, "there is probably some family rule that everyone hasta start smoking PMs at age thirteen."

"I just called Lynn on my cell," Ab said, "and she is over at the house now, so follow me."

We wound our way all around the huge Collier County and Australian pine trees, and then entered a five-acre oyster-shell covered flat area that I learned later had been dubbed Viking Country many years earlier. I followed Ab to a house sitting on top of some pilings. He parked near the stairs leading up, so I put mine beside his truck.

"C'mon up," Ab yelled and headed up the stairs.

"This's Lynn's father-in-law, Ray McMillin's house. His family, a grandfather I believe, came here from the Netherlands when he was young. Ray came down from Minnesota when he was a young guy and liked it here, so he bought property. He did carpenter work for a while and then later he started fishing for a living."

Abner stopped at the top on the landing where the main entry door was, and pointed out across Chokoloskee Bay. "Look at all that wilderness right here in our back yard." He shook his head as he scanned with his eyes, "Some deep-pockets boys from up north som'rs have been nosing around and talking about getting laws changed so they can begin developing some sections of those Ten Thousand Islands."

When Abner turned around toward me, his mouth was all shriveled up, "Shit! And the way things are these days the bastards will probably find a way."

"Yeah," I answered, "always the same ole shit, money talks and bullshit walks."

"Hi, Abner, is this the fella from Miami who wants to rent Ray's house?"

"Yeah, Lynn. "This is Engelburt Fetterman from Miami. Sounds like a Yankee, but he ain't. Walked out on his rich fat-cat banker daddy, and came down here to go to the University of Miami. He's a writer and is gonna do some writing about those damn pythons that're taking over our Everglades."

An attractive middle-aged lady opened the door and then stepped back, "C'mon in and have a look around, Engelburt."

"Just plain Burt, Lynn, and I don't really need to look around if you're busy, because this house will be perfect for my stay here in Chokoloskee."

"I'm done. C'mon, I'll show you the place real quick and then I've gotta run some errands."

~ O ~

Fifty-five miles away in a North Naples club named The Village Lounge, a pair of very dark complexioned men wearing extremely expensive silk suits, Gucci shoes, and custom mirrored designer sunglasses, sat in an isolated private booth talking.

"Everything going okay?" The swarthy man with the 24K gold rimmed shades said.

Jerome Sennitt smiled, "Sure is, Amad. My people in Miami are anxious to see the product, and if it's as pure as you say, they'll be able to pay cash for any amount you can supply them with."

"Very good," the other man replied. Both dark men were six-footers and very powerfully built. Four previous meetings with the two men, and Jerome still felt an evil power radiating from them.

"Jerome," Amad, obviously the head man, said, "your wife's family that still lives in Cuba is extremely well connected." He took a brief sip of his apricot brandy cocktail before speaking to Jerome again. "My associate," he nodded at the dark man sitting across from him, "Jintan, has family in Havana, and they know them quite well, even though they have never done any business together." He leaned back in his plush captain's chair to fish out a thin black cigarette from his solid gold case.

When Jerome, three months earlier, had met them through his

wife's cousin, he mentally separated them as Mister Gold and Mister Silver. Amad had gold frames on his dark glasses, gold cufflinks, gold tie pin, a gold case where he kept his foul-smelling cigarettes, and a gold Rolex. He had a gold money-clip thick with cash.

Jintan had silver duplicates of everything that Amad exposed for him to see. Jerome chuckled to himself when he was alone, following this fifth meeting with the two mysterious men. *I'll bet,* he thought, *they carry condoms in gold and silver tins.*

"Jintan's people in Cuba told him that they can be trusted." Amad turned toward Mister Silver, "Isn't that right, Jintan?"

"Yessir, they are quite well known in all the business circles that my family moves in, and all say they are solid reliable people to do business with."

The entire time he spoke, Jerome had the feeling that Mister Silver was simply repeating something that he had memorized earlier, and was working hard to bring the words forward.

Mister Gold leaned slightly forward, "Jerome, we have checked you out thoroughly and are very pleased with the results. The attache case I carried in this time has two hundred thousand dollars cash in it for you to move ahead now and begin setting up the operation that we discussed. It also has a half kilo of our product for you to show your people." He lifted the small round glass to his lips while watching Jerome. When he sat the glass down, Mister

Gold said, "We will leave now, but will remain in the car down the street to be sure you are not followed." He smiled for the first time since they had met, and Jerome saw that his two eye teeth were gold. "We'll meet at number six on your list in four weeks. We'll then see how everything is progressing."

The two men stood, and Mister Silver placed a pair of twenties on the table to cover the two cocktails and a beer that Jerome only drank half of.

As they walked out, Jerome paused to pick up the leather case and then slowly followed, thinking, *if Mister Silver ever smiles, I'll be surprised if he doesn't have silver eye teeth.*

~ O ~

One block south on Highway 41, a man was looking through powerful binoculars. He and another man were in room 402 of the Tamiami Hotel. He spoke softly to the seated man next to him with one of the earphones above his ear. "Alpha One and Alpha Two just left. Bravo One is outside now, and is carrying a briefcase."

The seated man was relaying the information into a tiny, wireless microphone clipped to his shirt collar.

"Alpha One and Alpha Two just entered their vehicle. Bravo One is standing next to his vehicle and is looking in every direction. Alpha One and Alpha Two are now driving south. Bravo One is in his vehicle but not yet moving. Alpha One and Alpha Two just pulled into the parking lot of The Conch Diner, but have not exited their vehicle. Bravo One is now pulling out onto Tamiami Trail to head south. Alpha One and Alpha Two are still in their vehicle. Bravo One just drove past The Conch Diner. Alpha One and Alpha Two have not moved. Bravo One is stopped at the traffic light. Alpha One and Alpha Two have pulled out and are following Bravo One a few vehicles back. Inform Crabtrap Two that we are losing them and to take up the surveilance."

A moment later the seated man lifted the earphones from his head. "They have them, Jack, let's go get som'n to eat."

"Yeah man, this has been a long night waiting on those pricks to show up."

~ O ~

Abner Brown slowed his aluminum airboat down after thirty minutes and let the aircraft engine idle. "Ever been in one of these, Burt?"

"Nope, and watching them roar across the Glades on TV doesn't give a person a clue how exhilarating it is." Engelburt shielded his eyes with his hand and scanned the area. "How fast were we going, Ab?"

"Fifty at three-quarter throttle, but she'll do seventy if I gotta get somewhere in a hurry."

Rick Magers

"You said everyone that had an airboat used to run all over these Everglades before the state and the feds put a stop to it?"

"Yeah, and it's good they did, because we were all too wrapped up in our own thing to give a shit how much damage we were doing to these Glades."

"How's that?" Burt turned to look up at Ab when he asked the question.

"Well," he paused to lift up his huge red and black checkered bandana to wipe sweat from his face, "many of us had hunting cabins scattered around out here. We'd locate a nice hammock that had some high ground, and then we'd just start clearing off a small area. Once we had a site ready, we would start cutting up the trees we'd chopped down. When we had us enough lumber split to frame out a cabin, we'd begin by digging a series of holes to set those framing posts in."

"What kind of trees did y'all use?"

"Cypress, mostly, cause there's so much of it, and it'll last when other wood rots. Lotta Collier County pine too."

"How big did you make the cabin?"

"Mine is eight feet square, but some guys went ape shit. One guy built himself a great big ole sprawling places with separate bedrooms for when they brought girls out here. One guy set up a permanent generator and even had a goddamn TV antenna on the roof." Abner shook his head, "Shit like that's what caused the

Everglades National Park Service to start enforcing laws already on the books, and creating new ones to keep assholes like that from turning these Glades into a new kinda tourist attraction."

"Your cabin is still out here, huh?"

"Yep, and ain't but a couple others in the whole damn Glades."

"How did you manage that?" Burt asked with a grin.

"Well," Abner wiped the sweat from his face again, "I built it up just a foot off the ground, 'cause the mound was pretty high, and the ceiling's only seven foot above the floor, like most houses used to be, so they'd be easier to heat in winter, and cool with fans in summer. That kept it pretty damn low. Then I used palmetto thatching for the roof to keep it from standing out when planes flew over. Used a come-along ratchet to pull two big gumbo-limbo trees over it to make the roof blend in even more." He grinned down at Burt, "It took a lotta lookin to find the right hammock that had everything I needed."

"I've heard that the Governor is a friend of yours."

Abner looked down through a wide grin. "People that have enough money tucked away in the bank to become the governor, president, or whatever, don't have common shit-between-their-toes country boys like me as their friend. Burt."

"But you know him pretty well, doncha?"

"M'dad knew Boyer Halsey pretty good back in them wild-ass eighties, so when Skip, his son, was running for governor he asked me to help put together an old fashion wild hog barbecue, with country music, hog-head stew, Indian fry bread, swamp cabbage, the works." Abner did a short pause recalling those good old days.

When, after a couple of minutes he didn't say a word, Engelburt said, "That what got him elected?"

"Well, Burt, I can't say it got him into the Governor's Mansion, but it sure as hell did not hurt. Hell's Belles, there were over five thousand people at that damn barby." He grinned down at me again, "And I think ever dern one of 'em voted for skip. We've been kinda close ever since."

~ O ~

Thirty miles southwest of where Engelburt and Abner sat talking in the airboat, Abner's cousin, Jake Brown, talked in his natural, swamp baritone voice, as he led his group deeper into the Everglades.

"Folks, Fakahatchee Strand has been home to purdy near every species of wildlife in these here Everglades for centuries." He continued to walk while pointing at birds and plants, "Those white Ibis y'all see near that pond, soon became known locally as our Chokoloskee Chickens. It was because they were deliscious and plentiful. Pioneers like my great-uncle, Totch's daddy, and all his neighbors lived off the land during all the years they called the Ten Thousand Island's home. They......

Rick Magers

Jake's new walking tour was becoming the most popular local attraction to all of the tourists that didn't mind roughing it for four hours. They usually left South Florida with a very thorough understanding of how and why the Everglades effected Southern Florida.

This trip however, would end considerably different than any other.

~ O ~

Abner Brown fired up the huge aircraft engine, and while the propellar was still turning slowly in the cage behind the high aluminum operator's seat, he leaned down and said loud enough for Engelburt to hear, "**Lean back in the seat and hold on.**"

Burt nodded and grabbed the handrails on each side of the fiberglass seat.

Thirty thrilling minutes for Burt later, the engine was again idling. "Wow," he looked up behind him, "Disney got one of these rides yet?"

"Nah," Abner grinned, "they're too damn busy makin dancing ducks and flying elephants, but I reckon they'll eventually have an airboat ride in Disneyworld Three, on Tamiami Trail."

Burt answered, "Don't remind me." He then looked at the hammock they had stopped near. "I reckon this here's the most beautiful hammock I've seen yet; looks like som'n you would see in a film shot in Africa. It must be where your cabin sits, huh?"

"Nope, mine's even prettier, but you'll never forget whacha see in there." Abner gave his boat a bit of throttle and moved toward a small opening in the dense foilage. Once he had the bow against the bushes, he gunned the Engine. The bow lifted, and Burt grabbed the armrests harder and leaned back.

Suddenly the bushes folded down as the up-sloping aluminum bow forced its way in. Burt's mouth dropped open as the airboat idled into a small clear lake that was completely hidden. He watched as Abner turned the bow towards the bushes that were still a bit folded down. He eased the bow into them and gently throttled the boat to return them to their normal position.

"Keep your eyes on the tree limbs, because there's about a hundred huge reticulated pythons that have laid eggs in here."

Burt turned to say something, but stopped when he saw that Abner was strapping on a holstered pistol and ammunition belt.

"I don't think any of these pythons will make a move toward us." Abner was standing up on his aluminum seat. He looked down and grinned, "They're too dern busy guarding their nests. But I figure mebbe someone, way back when, musta turned loose one of those damn anacondas, and I don't wanna be groping for this forty-four Dirty Harry when it pops up next to the boat."

"Holy shit, you got another one of those?" Burt used his chin to motion toward Abner's pistol.

"No, but I've been in this hammock quite a few times, so I sure doubt there's one around here." He lifted his chin, "See that big python moving up to a limb, gettin a better look at us?"

Burt quickly stepped up on his seat and leaned back against Abner's seat. Abner chuckled.

"Don't laugh, let's get the hell outa here."

"Don't panic, Burt, cause if there was a big anaconda anywhere around here, there'd be war going on. These pythons are as protective of their eggs as gators are. Back in twenty twelve," Ab crunched his eyebrows down, "or mebbe it was thirteen, the Park Rangers were called to get a seventeen and a half foot python that some folks in West Palm Beach spotted, and was keeping an eye on." He looked down at Burt, who had returned to his seat, "That's longer'n this damn boat. They found out later, when they cut her open, that she had eighty-seven eggs inside. They got a heavy wire loop over her head and six of 'em began dragging her out of a marshy swamp behind a trailer park. When she was up on dry land, that python began flipping herself over and over. She was trying to get a loop over anyone close to her. A coil was actually around one of the rangers that was knocked down, and she was about to get a second coil around the gal, when the head ranger shot it six times point blank in the head. That lady ranger said her ribs felt like she had been hit by a dumptruck. Burt, that sucker is a hundred n' sixty-some pounds or more."

Burt had stood briefly to look around with caution, but then he moved back down to the seat. His head however was in constant motion trying to see everything around the boat. "How big do the pythons get?"

"Biggest one ever caught was thirty-three feet, but a python that big is very rare. Usually they're about fifteen feet when they're full grown."

"Damn. How about those anacondas?"

I recently read where the biggest one ever caught was twenty-eight feet long, and had a forty-four inch girth. Those guys finally got it up onto the scale and it weighed a bit over five hundred pounds."

"Holy crap," Burt nodded toward Abner's big pistol, "And I reckon that forty-four's gonna stop som'n that big, huh?"

Abner grinned wide, "This forty-four magnum will stop almost anything out here."

"Almost anything, huh? What's out here that a couple of those forty-fours' wouldn't stop?"

"Y'ain't heard about the Skunk Ape?"

"Yeah, Maggie told me about Dave Shealeys', Skunk Ape."

"Burt," Abner had a serious look on his face when he said, "the Indians have been talking about a creature like that since long before Dave was born."

Rick Magers

He looked at Burt for a moment, before saying, "I brought you out here on purpose so you could see these bigass pythons. And I told you about the anaconda, so when you're with me in this airboat or riding up on my Swamp Castle, you'll know to be damned careful. If one of 'em ever gets a loop on either of us, it'll take both of us doing everything right, and be doing it damn quick." He turned and spit a stream of tobacco juice into the water. "If we don't act fast, one or both of us might be joining those damn pythons for lunch." He had a big grin now, "And guess what's for lunch?"

"You, because I'm half Jew, and Hitler found out we don't taste good when he tried feeding his troups real, hand-made, kosher sausages."

"Sorry Rabbi, these fokers always choose the small one." Ab's grin widened, "Big, ole hard-headed guys like me give them snakes hemorrhoids."

"What's your swamp castle?"

"You'll see it later, but for now we are gonna check another hammock."

~ O ~

Forty-five miles east, the two young boys from Miami Springs, Hialeahs' sister city over on the south side of the Miami River, were moving across the sawgrass in a new airboat. It was a sixteen-foot-long fiberglass hull, and was powered by a Porche air-cooled engine. It had a four-blade composit propellar, and ingnoring Ronnies plea to leave the big straight pipes on the engine, his father had mufflers installed.

"There's enough noise in this new world, son, so we'll not add to it."

Ronnie Weingartens' wealthy father had promised to buy him an airboat on his eighteenth birthday. A month earlier it had been delivered to their ten acre estate, The Weingarten Garden.

Ronnie completed a two-day course in Air Boat Safety at a man-made swamp ten miles north of his home. His entire life had been filled with boy-toys, from battery-powered sportscars, trucks, forklifts, and motorbikes. All went to the dump soon after Ronnie climbed on his first gasoline powered Honda dirt bike.

His sixteenth birthday party ended with Ronnie and his lifetime best friend, Ziggy Skatze, taking turns riding around his new oval course with rolling hills that were created just for the dirtbike. The other thirty guests were ignored.

His seventeenth birthday eclipsed all others when he saw the brand new 2019 Dodge Magnum-*PLUS* pickup truck being delivered on a flatbed. The white silk ribbon and bow on top made the coal-black metalic paint seem to shimmer even more.

"I had the brake pedal modified," his five-foot-tall father said, "exactly like I did mine, and the accelerator too. You can adjust the seat and reach them just fine."

The Dodge Ram easily towed the airboat to the launch ramp in a section of West Hialeah. The two boys parked the truck and trailer beside five other truck & trailer rigs that had already shed their airboats. Those men were already out roaring across the sawgrass. Ronnie removed his regular shoes, and pulled on his leather, custom-built 5" elevated boots. He had recently bought them at Jorge Gonzalez' Safari Outfitters in the Hialeah Mall. The moment he pulled them on, he thought, *the best eight hundred bucks I ever spent.*

Ronnie deftly flipped on his theft alert, which would summon a helicopter once they saw his father's name on the alert. One last look inside to be sure he had not left anything, and Ronnie locked the truck, then swaggered toward Ziggy, who was holding the bowline. Two short boys feeling better in each other's presence — one now five inches taller.

~ O ~

**A** very plain thirteen story building in West Ft. Myers had a minimum of windows, and all of them had Sun-Shield-99 on the outside to prevent unwanted eyes from reading lips through powerful telescopes.

Rick Magers

The drab old building now housed three extremely important departments involved in USA security. On the first three stories, there was a vast array of different functions that the FBI was engaged in 24/7, as was the NSA on the next three floors. INS occupied floors 7 through 9, but had better hours. The non-federal people worked 9 to 5 shifts, Monday thru Friday, and then returned to their own private, normal lives.

Floors 10 and 11 were both filled with the very latest super-computers. Floor 12 was a very plush, completely furnished apartment, where a computer technician was available on a 24/7 basis. A technician was there for 24 hours, then he was off duty 48 hours, and another technician began the next shift.

The 12th floor was also a conference room. It could seat a dozen men, and when necessary, feed them until a solution to the problem was found.

. The top floor, number 13, was security. A very small army of men holding Top Secret clearance maintained an array of the latest equipment. It was also a 24/7 operation, which was capable of monitoring calls coming in from agents across the globe. The material used to construct the building was such that even the best snooping equipment could not penetrate. Incoming calls were routed to floor 13 via satellite, and then they were forwarded to the appropriate agency. Outgoing calls had to be authorized by the commander of NORAD at Peterson Air Force Base, Colorado.

~ O ~

Samson Blackraven began his career with the CIA on the same day that he was discharged from the Air Force, after a very exciting twenty years in Military Intelligence. He was recruited by MI while still a college senior. Three years later, he was promoted to Captain, and seventeen years later was discharged as a Major General.

Samson Blackraven was a six-foot-six-inch-tall, 255-pound Native American member of the Seminole Tribe. His dark black pupils, when dilated were frightening if accompanied by a frown. Born in Miami Florida to very wealthy parents he began his education with a private tutor. With a persuasive personality at the age of twelve, Samson convinced his parents to allow him to attend a public school. He chose Hialeah Jr. High, where he excelled through 7th, 8th, and 9th grades.

A very affable and well-liked fifteen-year-old, Samson chose Miami High School. Graduating with honors as valedictorian, Samson entered the University of Miami as a political science major, minoring in sociology.

With outstanding grades in economics, mathematics, biology, and psychology, he carried a Masters Degree into the military with him. Continuing his education online during twenty years in the military, he was honorably discharged as Dr. Samson Blackraven, PhD. USAF Ret., wearing two stars.

In March 2000, Samson was given the task of creating a brand new bipartisan command building where the CIA, NSA, and INS could monitor and maintain the security of the United States of America in South Florida.

That huge unpretentious building in West Ft. Myers became known as The Fort.

The men who had begun their careers at this unique monolith, which by the way was actually created by their boss, considered themselves lucky.

His earliest crew had dubbed Samson, Chief, and it stuck. The single-word title's origin was not at all due to his ethnicity, but rather his unique ability to evaluate any and all situations quickly and issue orders to the men he felt certain could get the job done.

Agent Pablo Garcia pressed the star button on his desk's intercom. It connected him to Samson's desk. "Chief, I just got a message from Bravo-One that I think you oughta look at."

A second after lifting his finger, the Chief's deep voice came from the speaker. "Bring it in, Pablo."

~ O ~

75-year-old Sheenie Goldberg, known to everyone in the two small towns, and Plantation, an island settlement you enter after crossing a bridge opposite Airport Road......as **Jungle Jew**. Sheenie was intently listening to someone on the phone, as a frown grew across his face.

His 81-year-old sister, Julie, frowned when he yelled into the phone, "I don't give a dead rat's ass if he has the goddamned Governor's ear. My nephew Abner has his home and cell phone numbers, and the goddamned guy even flies down from Tallahassee every time Ab has a cookout." He held the old-fashioned black telephone out in front of him as though he wanted to either strangle it or throw it against the wall. He took a deep breath before screaming into the phone, "**So go call him**." He slammed the phone down and mumbled a few expletives that made Julie cringe—again.

"You should not blaspheme like that, Sheenie." Julie had a tinny voice that was now also just a wee bit shaky.

Julie's tall skinny carcass did not appear durable enough to prevent her frail bones from being pushed on through the paper-thin skin. However, even as a kid, there had always been a scary gleam in her eyes that worried her brother.

'If you were a goddamn Catholic visiting the Vatican,' he mumbled softly, 'the goddamn Pope would get pissed off and have you thrown out.'

"What?" Julie asked her brother in a strained falsetto voice while staring at him through diamond-hard eyes.

"Nothing!" *That old bat can hear a saber tooth gnat fart.* "You're absolutely right. I just get fed up with assholes like that." *Like I am with you,* he thought.

Julie just shook her head and continued crocheting. A few stitches later she asked, "Was that about making the airboats quieter?"

It irritated Sheenie that his sister could always figure out who he was talking to on the phone. "Howja guess?"

"Nobody gets you riled up like Phyllis MacAllenby."

He pulled out the bottom left drawer of his desk and retrieved the ever-present bottle of scotch. Sheenie bolted down a three-finger shot and filled the glass again before returning the bottle and shoving the drawer in. Once his nerves settled down, he pivoted the chair and spoke in a softer voice. "Why do those fat snow buzzards come down here to the swamp and then try to turn it into the shithole they left behind?" He shook his head and then sipped the scotch.

Julie shook her head, pinched her lips, closed both eyes, and emitted a long sigh, but said nothing about her brother's foul language. After a moment she said, "She's been living here on the Barron River in that house for ten years, Sheenie."

"So what, you and I been living in this house on the river for over forty, and we ain't trying to change nothing at all." *At least I'm not.* He thought.

Rick Magers

"She's still mad about you giving everyone with a Florida tag one of those bumper stickers you had made."

Sheenie laughed and emptied his glass. "Don't feed the snow buzzards and they'll go home." He pulled the drawer back out and grabbed the scotch. "I just ordered another five hundred to hand out to Floridians at the Seafood Festival this season." He emptied the glass again and refilled it. "I hope Abner can convince the governor to squash the bill that damn Phyllis is trying to get passed that'll make all airboats owners get those special new mufflers that some asshole at Yale invented."

"They're too loud the way they are now, Sheenie."

Sheenie had started to say something about how they caused the airboats to run slower and even damaged the engines after a while. He saw her turn the icy, diamond-hard stare toward him, so he gulped down the scotch and stormed out of the house before he said something he would regret.

~ O ~

Jake Brown's Everglades Walking-Tour group, on this beautiful cloud-free, sunny day, was still having the time of their lives. They were at the halfway mark of his short, half-day walk, three miles into the Fakahatchee Strand. The group of twenty had entered the swamp at 7:00 AM, and now at 10:00 AM it was time for an energy snack.

Each person who signed up for the Everglades walk had been given a cloth-bound, one-quart plastic canteen attached to a webbed stretch-belt, with a logo advertising his Swamp Walk. Jake passed out the energy bars. As they chewed and drank, Jake pointed out several small orchids and air plants that were indigenous to this area of the Everglades.

Only one of the three men, who had accompanied the seventeen women on the tour bus from Orlando, was a bit overweight. He was leaning back against a huge old cypress tree, and while gasping, was wiping sweat off his bald head and red face.

Jake approached him silently, and took his flowered shirt in his hand and pulled the bulgy little man away from the tree. Before the man could speak, Jake pointed and said, "Even non-poisonous snakes can be deadly if they startle you."

"**Snake**?" the man screamed, leaping away. Jake still had a wad of shirt in his hand, and prevented the man from falling into the water.

Jake reached up to the low-hanging vine and let the snake slither down his arm and onto his shoulder. "This is a young King Snake, and it can be a blessing to have one decide to live under or around your house. They are not poisonous and will kill and eat any other snakes that invade its territory." He looked at the fat man, who had his mouth open so wide, that his uppers were about to fall out.

"A rattler or even a cottonmouth is no match for this fella," he reached up and let the young snake come down his bare arm, "once he's come full grown."

"How about all of those pythons we've been hearing about?" the fat little man asked.

"A King Snake," Jake said, "would be no match for a python, but the news media is exaggerating the amount of them in the Everglades." Jake walked back to the limb and coaxed the snake to move back up into the foliage.

Turning back to his group, he said, "Time now for us to begin the second half of today's walking tour." He pointed toward a sturdy cypress bridge that crossed a twenty-foot wide flow of water. "We'll cross over to the return trail, and with any luck," he turned toward the group and let them all see his beaming smile, "We'll see a few more species of wildlife, but no more snakes."

~ Simple wishes—often ignored by the gods ~

Thirty-five miles northeast, those very same two young boys who went into the Eastern Everglades in the new airboat, were now cautiously moving into the huge hammock. Careful not to knock his canvas jungle hat off, Ziggy was bent to almost double with his hand holding the hat to his curly red hair.

Ziggy held the top of the croaker sacks that rested on his shoulder and hung down his back. His other hand, on the artificial bone handle of his Chinese, Tarzan machete.

Ronnie could not see very well while looking through his new expensive, Oakley polarized sunglasses, under the dense ceiling growth, but knew he really looked cool, so he left them on.

He had seen some cool guys on TV shows that put the hat strap under their chin when stalking through jungle growth, just as he was doing now, so he had done the same before they entered.

An hour later, they walked out of the dense growth to find themselves standing on the edge of a dry, football-field-size opening. Both boys unsnapped and removed their plastic canteens from the flimsy sheath on their belt.

After drinking half of their tepid water, the two boys proceeded around the north edge.

"How much do you think we'll get for live pythons?"

Ronnie stopped and pushed his hat back a bit, and as he surveyed the area, spoke to Ziggy. "Well Zig, I read an article just last week that stated a zoo somewhere up north, I forget which one, paid a guy five grand for a six footer."

"Wow, we've brought ten gunny sacks. So," he took a moment to calculate, "if we fill each one with a python we'll have, uh, about, mmm…a good payday."

Rick Magers

"Yeah boy," Ronnie said as he pulled his hat off and rubbed his kinky black hair, "we might have found the path to independent wealth before we've even figured out which college we're going to."

"Betcha," Ziggy said enthusiastically, "we can hire Og and Boliver Kollesio. They could use their rich father's airboat to catch a shitload of pythons for us."

Ronnie put his hat back on and shook his head. "Yep, they're both reliable, and smart enough that I could teach 'em how to catch and handle snakes. Might take a few weekends though because they're always arguing about one thing or another." He pinched his lips and leaned his head back, "Morgan would be a really good man to have on our team too. He's got plenty of guts, plus his dad's already taught him how to run his airboat. "I'll be able to teach him how to catch these pythons in a weekend or two."

As the two boys proceeded around the perimeter of the huge hammock, their heads were filling with dreams of a fleet of airboats and a huge Miami office overlooking Biscayne Bay.

Half way around, Ziggy pointed down at an eight-inch-deep concave impression at the edge of the dry mound. The terrain had changed into a soft muddy stretch of land leading into the swamp. "Ronnie, y'gotta see this track." Ziggy yelled.

After inspecting the track, Ronnie walked back and forth for a few minutes. Finally returning, he pursed his lips again and shoved

65

his jungle hat back before saying, "It looks t'me like someone has been cutting down trees and dragging them somewhere to build a cabin on this dry mound."

"Yeah, that's what I figured, too." Ziggy looked down at the track again. "Yep, it's about the size of the trees they use to build 'em."

"Damn," Ronnie said loudly, "bad for us."

Ziggy scrunched his eyebrows down, and tried hard to understand why it was bad for them. Finally giving up on it, he asked, "Why?"

Ronnie twisted his lips and swiveled his head around to survey the entire hammock they were hunting in. His first word came stretched out with a very long sigh. "Weeeeeeeeeell, I reckon with all the activity of cutting logs and dragging them out of the way until they'll be needed, there won't be any pythons here."

Ziggy shook his head of curly red hair, "Yeah, that's what I was thinking too. Guess we oughta just move on to another hammock.

"Yep, might's well." Firming his jungle hat back on his head and putting the strap beneath his chin, Ronnie handed Ziggy the python catchpole. Ziggy slung it over his shoulder and followed Ronnie back the way they had come. Without turning, Ronnie said, "I'm ready for a sandwich and a nice cold Coke to wash down this bitter disappointment, before we head off looking for another hotspot."

Rick Magers

"Me tooooooooo," Ziggy hooted, "I'm hoooongry."


~ Youthful ignorance and hasty decisions — often fatal ~


~ O ~

To the west, a sixth meeting between Mister Gold, and Mister Silver, was taking place at St. George & The Dragon, a classy dinner house at the edge of Old Naples, with Jerome Sennitt.

Once they had placed their dinner orders, Amad put his arms on the table to lean over and speak to Jerome, "I hope everything has been taken care of for our upcoming event." His gold-tooth smile still appeared evil to Jerome and sent a cold chill running up his spine, as though tiny mice with frozen feet had suddenly been released.

Jerome smiled and answered softly, "Everything is on track and will be ready and waiting."

"And one of the airboat operators you have chosen," Amad asked, "is also a good mechanic in case one of the engines needs repair?" It seemed to Jerome that Amad's smile was tattooed on his face.

"Yes, Amad, and he's already putting together a box full of the items that he feels could fail, like spark plugs, magnetos, spare fuel hoses and oil lines." He took a calming sip of his Manhattan, and then added, "He saved a load once a few years ago, when we brought in one from Colombia in a shrimper. I don't know much about diesels, but he kept it running until we offloaded the three thousand pounds of cocaine and the three of us got onto the go-fast boats, and then sunk the old bitch."

Amad's smile softened up a bit, "Sounds like a good man to have around."

"He is," Jerome whispered, "he's my brother-in-law and we've worked together quite a few times, so I know I can trust him."

"Good," Amad said softly while nodding slightly at Mister Silver, who always sat beside Jerome. "Jintan is also my brother-in-law, and we've worked together for thirty years. Ah, here is our dinner."

They parted after eating. Jerome left first, and fifteen minutes later, the two swarthy men sauntered out.

Jerome drove toward his seafood market & restaurant that was a mile beyond The Village Lounge. *At times I wish I had never gotten involved with those two.* His mind was in a turmoil as he drove north on US 41. *If I can get through this alive, it'll be the last time. I'll go straight and build up my market. My deal with Blackraven to keep the CIA informed will wipe my record clean.* He pulled a half-full pint of Jack Daniels out from under his seat and took a long pull before replacing it.

"Jintan," Amad said; driving east on Tamiami Trail toward the huge warehouse and office in Southwest Miami, "please catch a plane tonight to Barranquilla and be certain that all is ready for our planned operation. The very minute the plane comes to rest in the swamp, and our five men are on each airboat, they are to kill those five drivers and toss the bodies over. They can use the GPS in their Smart Phones to come straight to the area where you, our vehicles, and I are waiting. Omar will have already engaged the timer that will detonate the bomb placed in the airplane. The pilots should be about half way to Cuba when it blows up. The minute you inform me that our men are on the airboats, I will kill that fool, Jerome, and head toward the area where our men are waiting for the airboats. You should be there by then, Jintan, to oversee the loading of all the equipment into the motorhome."

"They must get all ten of those boxes on the airboats quickly. I have told Omar that they are all full of very sensitive electronic components, and they are all to be handled carefully." Amad glanced left at Jintan, "I hope he has told his men to be very, very, careful." With a big grin, he added, "I could rest easy if I knew that you were there instead of Omar, but I would be very lost, my dear friend, without you nearby to assist me."

Allah has been with us so far," Jintan said, "and I feel that his presence is with us every moment of every day." He turned his cruel chiseled face toward Amad. "Brother, Allah will stand beside us all the way as we teach these infidels a lesson that will certainly make Brother Osama's twin towers strike, seem like mere child's play."

~ O ~

The two men wearing earphones glanced at each other and smiled. They remained a good distance behind and continued listening as their quarry drove along the Trail toward Krome Avenue. There, the terrorists would turn south toward Homestead and intersect US 1, and then head east to their warehouse. "Chief," the older man said, "has already located the only place these guys could ever get a vehicle in to offload the airboats, in case the SEAL team runs into problems."

"Who did he bring in for that?"

"Chief called NORAD and convinced the General that a second SEAL team should be set up there and remain hidden, just in case."

The younger man chuckled softly, "If for some damn reason the SEALS driving the airboats toward those two Hummers at the drop zone ain't wearing red SEAL shit, their day ain't gonna end well at all. I don't know what it is, but I do know it only glows when seen through a SEAL night-vision scope."

"Don't worry about those SEAL guys, because they know to dot every I and cross every T before they begin a new phase of an operation."

"I sure hope so."

Rick Magers

"Count on it. My brother's been a Navy SEAL for ten years."

~ O ~

Amad glanced over at Jintan, "While you are in Colombia, I will double check that the men are ready to secure the landing so the airboats can quickly get those ten crates of ours into the two Hummers." He glanced again at his silent partner, "You are very quiet tonight. Is everything okay with you, brother?"

"Yes, brother, I have been praying to Allah quite a lot lately." Jintan turned toward Amad and smiled, "He is going to help us in our quest to run these American Infidels from our land forever."

"I know how efficient you are, but I must stress again the importance that the aircraft is loaded and ready, and will depart at the exact moment I specified."

"Allah and I will see to it."

"Good. Please return as soon as you have everything and everyone ready. You, brother, are the only man that I can trust to do everything that I ask."

Jintan turned and smiled, "Amad, I will always do everything that I can to justify the faith that you and Allah have placed in me."

~ O ~

$A$t The Fort, Samson Blackraven saw the expression on his agent,

Pablo Garcia's face as he approached his all-glass office. He motioned Pablo in before the agent even had a chance to knock.

He had worked with Pablo while they were both still in the Air Force. Samson knew that he was a stickler for protocol and he seldom encouraged any of his agents to step outside of that rigid box. However, this case was becoming too critical to allow protocol to interfere with national security.

He leaned back in his chair and listened intently.

"Chief," Garcia said before he even sat down in one of the chairs, "your gamble paid off in blue chips. Bravo-One, just a few moments ago, relayed to us all of that new information you had hoped he would."

Samson pursed his lips while nodding slowly up and down. "Took a lot of surveillance, but if those bastards could be lucky enough to get away with som'n like this it could be a blow that even America would have a hard time overcoming." His jet-black pupils shined like a new eight ball momentarily, but just as quick, they softened as he leaned forward to smile at his best agent, "Good job, PG." Samson's eyes hardened again, "Keep all your best men on this, because if their cargo is what we believe it is, I'll move it up from Operation Sparkle to Shine." He grinned as Garcia stood, "And then your guys'll stay so close they will know whether or not these guys lift the seat before pissing."

Samson reached out and pressed button 13, the only red one on his telephone console. "Please connect me to the commander at NORAD." He did not have to introduce himself because all internal calls were made via recording video.

He leaned back thinking about Operation Swamprat. *I am glad the one they sent to Israel was a dud, because now we know what we're dealing with.*

"Hello again, General Masterson," Chief sat up and leaned toward the video console, "all with Operation Swamprat is moving ahead and we'll soon have the ETD and ETA of the aircraft."

"Very good, Samson. Thanks a lot for keeping me updated as it moves along. I'll notify you the moment that I learn when SEAL teams seven and eight are headed your way. Over and out."

The screen went blank and Samson leaned back. *Gotta stay on top of this one*, he thought, *because the future of this country will be bleak if we drop the ball for just a second.*

~ O ~

Sixty miles and one hour later, Abner Brown stopped the huge airboat by idling the airplane engine. They were about a football field distance from one of the smaller hammocks. While the engine sputtered along slowly on idle, Abner scanned the dense foilage with his powerful binoculars. Burt's head was in full swivel as he tried to keep watch on all of the water around the airboat.

Five minutes later, Abner shoved the glasses back into their fiberglass waterproof case and bumped the throttle enough to cause the airboat to move slowly toward the thick mangroves.

Burt didn't see the narrow wooden walkway until the bow of the airboat almost touched it. When Abner shut the engine off, and told him to tie the bow line to a stout mangrove, Burt said, "I didn't see the walkway until we almost touched it."

Abner stood and climbed down from the aluminum seat tower and grinned, "That wasn't an accident, Burt."

"You built it, huh?"

"Yep, and every now n' then I carry out a small can of brown, and a small can of green latex paint with me to touch up the last few yards as I head back to the boat."

"That's pretty damned smart," Engelburt said, while looking at the camouflaged, eighteen-inch-wide wooden walkway that snaked through the mangroves, and then on into the hammock. "Why didn't you make it straight? Seems like it would have been a whole lot easier."

"Yeah, you're right, it would have been a whole lot easier, Burt. But because there's nothing out here in these Everglades that's straight, it would have stood out like a hooker at a Nun's birthday party."

Rick Magers

"Hmmm," he thought about it a moment, "yeah, that makes sense. We going in to look around?"

"Yep, I have a small nursery set up here, and on a few of the other small hammocks, too."

"Nursery! Whacha growing?"

"Snakes! C'mon, follow me." Abner stepped off of the airboat and onto the walkway and headed in.

Burt grabbed his Army/Navy Store webbed belt that came with a plastic canteen and a Chinese sheath-knife, and leaped onto the walkway too. His eyes never left the area his feet were touching as he strapped on the knife and canteen. He hurried along so he could catch up with Abner.

"Holy shit," he yelped like a startled dog.

Abner stopped and turned around to see Burt's arms flailing like a man about to fall off a tall building. "Whaja find, Burt?" he said, followed by a chuckle, "one of our swamp monsters?"

After frantically pulling off the sticky spiderweb, Burt stepped back and pointed at a small but vicious-looking black and white spider that had six pointed red spines sticking out. The small creature was scrambling up what was left of the web it had painstakenly created. "That creepy little bastard looks as if it could kill an elephant if it wanted to." Burt looked at Abner with stretched-wide, panicky eyes, "Is that thing venomous?"

"All spiders are venomous, Burt, but only a few inject a venom that is harmful to humans. That little bugger is a spiny orb weaver, but most everybody around here calls 'em a crab spider. If one hits you I don't reckon you're gonna live long enough to get to a hospital that has the anti venom." He kept a straight face while saying it.

"Holey shit." Burt stepped back as he rubbed his head to rid himself of the remaining web. "How do you know when one of the little bastards has bit you?" He was now looking at the web woven around both hands.

"They only bite someone that carelessly stumbles into their beautiful web, rather than stooping down a bit to go under it."

Burt was now wiping down both arms and trying to do the Exorcist maneuver with his head, so he could check his back.

Abner could no longer hold back his laughter, and burst out as he leaned over and rested both hands on his knees while trying to catch his breath.

Burt stopped and watched a moment. "I bet you were the unequaled class clown, werencha?"

Abner grinned, "Gotta have a little fun now n' then."

An hour later the two men had checked the eggs in two nests and were moving through a dense area toward a third, when Burt yelled, "Damn, look at the size of that cottonmouth," and pointed down at Ab's left foot."

A lightning-fast glance at Burt's pointing finger and Abner was leaping back toward Burt. When he couldn't see the snake Abner looked up at Burt beneath scrunched eyebrows.

Burt grinned, "Gotta have a little fun now n' then."

Abner just puckered up his lips and shook his head. His face then opened with a wide grin, "Touché amigo, y'got me, but let's call it even and stop doin it before one of us gets in a jam. That damn cry-wolf thing could kill us all, out here amongst these damn pythons."

Fifty feet later they were up on another walkway that ended at an elevated area that was dry. Burt followed Abner to the center of a one-acre clearing that was three feet higher than the surrounding mangroves. "I never would have expected to see anything like this," Burt said as he slowly turned all the way around. "Almost looks man-made."

"I reckon it is. My guess is that the Calusa Indians carried oystershell to some of the small hammocks to create a bunch of these raised areas. They were known as the people of the Caloosahatchee culture, and lived in settlements around Ft. Myers Beach, and also along the Caloosahatchee River, which is not far from here." Abner slowly turned 360 degrees, using his swamp-sharpened vision to be sure there was nothing to be concerned about before continuing. "About twelve thousand years ago the Paleo-Indian tribes moved into this area, so it mighta been them that first started building up all of these dry mounds. The Calusa were pretty thick around this area in the fifteenth century, so they probably stumbled across these dry mounds, and hundreds of 'em began hauling in canoe loads of oystershell to raise 'em on up higher."

"You're pretty damn good at the history of this area, Ab. I did quite a bit of research before heading here, but I would have never guessed that the ancient people who settled this area would have enhanced all these small hammocks like this. Why did they?"

"Well Burt," Abner said as his eyebrows scrunched down, "I ain't sure we'll ever really know, but they were a, uh, how should I say it, a very uh, a very superstitious people. These high dry areas mighta been created for specific religious uses, like a sacrifice to the wind gods, when the hurricanes came roaring through here." Abner looked around again before continuing, "I suppose it coulda been a place for a shaman to bring a new bunch of young boys that were about to undergo the ritual to become men, or warriors, or whatever."

"Yeah," Burt agreed, "there's no end to what they might have been created for, so you're right." He looked all around at the dry mound, "We'll probably never know the real reason."

~ O ~

Ronnie climbed up into the seat sitting on top of a six-foot-high aluminum frame. After starting the engine, he nodded to Ziggy, who coiled the rope and climbed in. Ronnie had driven his next-door neighbor, Bill's, airboat a few times when he was invited to ride along with him. Mister Hobart pointed out some of the ways a driver can get into a serious situation with an airboat. Ronnie listened intently whenever the old man spoke—he figured Mister Hobart was wise, because he was old like his father, who was thirty-eight.

Ziggy had the mental apparatus of a twelve-year-old. He continuously held his arm up motioning for Ronnie to go faster. Ronnie loved speed, whether on his dirt bike, in his truck, or driving across the sawgrass like now. However, when he felt the urge to bump the airboat throttle ahead a bit, he recalled Mister Hobart's words, and left it alone.

When Ziggy dug a Coke from the ice chest, Ronnie tapped him on the shoulder with the toe of his $800 Tony Lama, lizard skin, elevated jungle boots. Watching where he was going, Ronnie held his hand out while he opened and closed it a few times.

Ziggy yelled, "What?" several times before Ronnie put his hand to his lips as though drinking. "Oh," Ziggy yelled, and dug a Coke out of the ice and handed it up.

One hour later, Ronnie pulled the throttle back as he eased the boat toward a large hammock.

"You been to this one before, Ronnie?"

Rick Magers

"Nope!"

"Are we gonna tie up and see if we can find us a few of those damn pythons?"

"Yeah, but I'm gonna idle around it and see if there's a better place to tie up and scout around inside this hammock." Ronnie located a spot where the nose of the airboat could ease in under power far enough for them to step off onto dry land.

Once the boat was secured well to the mangroves, Ronnie said, "Strap your machete on tight, Ziggy, and secure the rawhide tong at the bottom of the sheath to your leg so it doesn't flop around." He watched Ziggy as he strapped on his own machete and then secured it to his leg. "Yeah man, that looks good. You carry the sacks and I'll bring the loop-stick I built."

Ziggy watched as Ronnie untied the lines that held the six-foot-long aluminum tubing that he had fashioned into a snake lariat after one he saw on Animal Kingdom.

"Hold your arm out, Ziggy, so I can test this, one last time before we go after 'em."

His friend complied, and Ronnie reached out with the loop-stick. The 3/16th inch stainless steel cable looped over Ziggy's wrist easily. The other ends of the cable were clamped to a round wooden handle, so all he had to do was pull on the handle while holding the aluminum tube, and the coil snugged up to Ziggy's wrist.

Rick Magers

"Pretty cool, man," Ziggy said as he admired his best friend's new invention. When the loop was removed, Ziggy put on his new African Safari White Hunter canvas jungle hat, and watched as his friend adjusted his. Ziggy had an unlimited debit card, so he had bought each of them one of the $189.99 hats.

Ronnie had recently bought himself a pair of $150 Oakley Polarized Frogskin Sunglasses, so Ziggy bought a pair too.

They both stepped out of the airboat looking like two kids on a Sesame Street Safari.

~ O ~

Abner motioned with his head, "C'mon, Burt, let's go have a look at the crop we're gonna get rich on."

Walking across the clearing, Burt asked Abner, "How many nurseries have you got out here?"

"Thirty, but I might hafta cut back to about twenty or twenty-five because it's almost more than just one guy can handle, even with a good helper."

They reached the edge of a clearing as Abner pointed his finger at a small bushy area at the base of a huge cypress tree. "I can see a few of the eggs, so mama must be keeping the enemy away from the nest."

"Wildlife here in the Glades must raise hell with any eggs they come across, huh?"

Abner grinned, "Actually they're just sorta like the bait to get mama a nice meal now n' then. A cunning fox or mebbe a sharp alert raccoon might get an egg now n' then. However, Burt, these mamas are coiled around the eggs every minute of every day, except when she uncoils to stretch out nearby in the sun to rejuvenate her heating system. She has gotta keep the temperature of the eggs very close to eighty-nine degrees for the entire eighty-five days of incubation. Just about the time ole Dopey Opossum decides that nobody's watching, he makes his move, probably thinking, oh boy, fresh eggs for lunch. Wham!" Abner held up his left fist and rushed in with his right to make three loops around it. "Mama has been nearby all the time stretched out to raise her temperature, but has been keeping an eye on everything. She lunges at ole Dopey like a bolt of lightning, and has the opossum in her jaws, and it'll soon be all wrapped up and crushed for lunch."

Burt moved closer to Ab, "You mean t'say that damn python is watching us right now?"

"Damn sure is pal, twenty-four seven until her babies are out, and ready to fend for themselves." He looked at Burt. "Don't worry; she's used to me coming by to have a look at her kids."

"So you're saying she thinks you are one of the good guys, huh?"

"Not really, but somehow she knows that man is her only real enemy out here, so she keeps her cool when we're around her eggs. Once they hatch and go on their way, then she'll take on anything that she thinks will fit in her belly, because after the three-month-watch over her eggs, she's ready to eat." Abner wobbled his eyebrows up and down, "Anything."

"How do you get the snakes when they come out of the shell without mama giving you a big hug? Your last one."

"I know within forty-eight hours when they're gonna start comin out, so I tie up at whichever hammock it is and get my gear ready. If it's a small batch, say twenty or so, and I get to 'em late, and they're starting to break out of the shell, I just bag 'em as they come out and then deliver all of 'em to a licensed research outfit in Miami. They meet me wherever the closest place is for me to dock, and they arrive in a van modified to hatch the eggs or just cage the babies. I looked it over real good before signing the contract, and it's all set up with the latest incubators inside cages." Abner nodded, "A real slick operation."

"How big is a large batch?"

"Biggest I've had was ninety-one, but they can lay well over a hundred."

"How the heck do you get the eggs without mama putting the squeeze on you?"

"I have a pet python that I bring with me, and she can handle anything that interferes with business."

Rick Magers

Abner's mischievous grin caused Burt's eyebrows to scrunch down. "Pet snake huh?"

"Nope, I said pet python. I'll show you later."

A while later, when they were back in the boat, Abner lifted the lid on a large fiberglass box that was bolted to the frame, below the binocular box. "I consider this baby my own personal American Express Card; I don't leave home without her."

Abner lifted the pistol up so Burt could see it, and then returned it to the padded fiberglass box. "My Uncle Sheenie ordered it in 2005. It's a Colt .357 Python hunting pistol that came with a 2X Leupold, factory installed scope. Unk took it off n' gave it to a pal of his that goes hunting up in British Colombia. He gave me the pistol three years ago. It almost broke his wrist when he went to the shooting range in Naples." He grinned and added, "I think he's actually afraid he'll shoot his sister that lives with him." He shook his head, "They argue all the time. His house is on the Barron River, so when he gets his fill of Aunt Julie, he goes to his pal, Orlo Hilton's restaurant, and sits in the office and has a few drinks to calm down."

"That's Triad, isn't it? The restaurant on the water that you pointed out, right across from the school."

"Yeah, I eat there often, because everything is always fresh, and you'll never hafta mortgage the boat to pay your bill, regardless

Rick Magers

what you order. I've been trying to get Orlo to put python on the menu, but I reckon he's gonna retire soon and move back to Immokalee."

"Damn, I didn't know they were edible."

"Hell yes they are, and their meat too is really good. Some other countries have been eatin' 'em for a hundred years, or probably a lot longer. I could sell ten times as much as I bring in."

"So, you get paid by the head from the state, and then you sell the meat too."

"Yep, and the skins too, that's why I have the Python pistol. I have it in my hand ready to fire when I come to collect the eggs. Mama knows I'm doin som'n different, so she lifts up to have a look-see, and that's when I put three of my bullets right in her head."

"Ouch," Burt groaned.

"Yeah, it sounds kinda cruel until you think about all of the Everglades wildlife she's eaten in the many years that she's been cruising around out here." Abner turned to look into Burt's eyes, "She's only one of maybe three or four hundred thousand. Those pythons have been out here for over fifty years, since people started keeping them as pets—until they got too big. They've been eating our deer, bear, panther, raccoon, opossum, alligator, crocodile, and anything else they see. They especially like bird eggs, so eventually that'll be the end of birds in the Glades, too."

Rick Magers

"Burt," he turned to look straight at him, "you're not from here, so you probably haven't noticed." He looked up through the canopy at the sky, and then turned all the way around again. "Ain't hardly any birds left; oughta be a hundred or two right here in this little hammock. If we don't start getting ahead of these damn snakes right soon, there ain't gonna be any birds left." Looking out through the thick mangroves with air plants and orchids hanging everywhere, he shook his head slowly. "If those damn fools in DC and Tallahassee woulda just put a high bounty on the pythons twenty years ago, when we first warned 'em, I reckon we would already be ahead of the snakes, and some of the wildlife would be building their numbers back up again."

Burt could see the pain on Abner's face and hear the disgust in his voice when he added, "This little paradise that God set aside, just for us, will soon be nothing but a snake refuge that won't be safe to come into. Really gets to me whenever I think about how this unique place of beauty is being handled."

Abner did not talk a lot, so Engelbert waited silently to see if he had more on his mind.

Finally he continued. "Burt, I'm sure you know that these Everglades are a one of a kind; none anywhere else on earth. Most folks probably think every country has an Everglades or som'n like this." He shook his head, "We all knew, all of us that is, that's been running around out here in our airboats a while, that when they

Rick Magers

put a regular road across from Lauderdale to Naples it was the beginning of the end for the Glades."

"Alligator Alley, y'mean?"

"Yeah, it's I-75 now." He turned toward Burt, "Before they first started hauling fill in to create Alligator Alley, some very knowledgeable people, engineers and others, told 'em not to do it because it would kill the Everglades. They told 'em to put the road up on pilings like they did in Louisiana when they put the first road across the bayous. They ignored 'em all and put in the road with a few culverts for water to pass through. This new I-75 has run-through areas too, but it is still not allowing the water to keep moving like the river of grass it was created to be. Those few run-throughs are just a bandage to make folks think everything's all right. It's about the same, I reckon, as a Band-Aid on a twenty-millimeter canon round in the chest. People lookin on see the medic putting it on, and they think it's gonna help, but he knows the guy's gonna die, sure's shit stinks." Burt watched as Abner rotated his head slowly—saying almost reverently. "We ain't gonna have this paradise much longer."

Burt sat there quietly, saying nothing for a couple of minutes, but then asked, "How do you keep the python meat from spoiling before you get it to the buyer?"

"I'll bring you along on my Swamp Castle when I come out to get a load, day after tomorrow. You will see it all then, but we are

Rick Magers

heading back now so I can make a few repairs on her."

As Burt followed Abner he asked, "How long before those eggs we just saw will hatch?"

Without turning, Abner said, "Seventeen or eighteen days, according to my log. I have two big batches of eggs in a hammock just over yonder." He kept on walking but pointed north, "Oughta get us about a hunert and fifty eggs and mebbe two, pretty good size snakes."

~ O ~

Jake Brown's walking-tour group was crossing over the small creek running beneath the wooden bridge. Jake led the group from the front, and kept them all informed of interesting flora and fauna by speaking into a small but powerful microphone. His voice came out of a small hi-tech, amplified speaker built into the rear of his fiberglass hat. The twentieth passenger could hear him clearly just as the one behind Jake, as long as each person did exactly what he or she was told, and remained one arm-length from the person in front.

The twentieth passenger on this tour was eighty-eight pound Sybil Schwat. Not counting her bouffant blonde wig, seventy-two-year-old Sybil Schwat stood four-foot-six-inches tall in her bare feet, and had never reached a hundred pounds.

After a lifetime of spending long hard hours in the Granite Bend

Public Library in Northern Montana as librarian, Sybil did not care a bit what kind of weather followed whatever outdoors guided tour she had booked. She had a mini-umbrella and a rain suit that was no larger than a cigarette pack. Her size four hiking boots were custom made, due to their small size, and were as waterproof as those worn by Army Rangers.

She strutted along carrying her all-weather backpack, just as proud as she still carried her spinster virginity. Each time a new bird was announced by Jake, Sybil stopped briefly to lift up the binoculars hanging around her neck. The eleven-hundred-dollar glasses had a tiny Nikon digital camera built in, so all she had to do once she had the bird or whatever it was in the viewer and centered, was touch a button. Since retiring at sixty-five, Sybil had filled nineteen albums with exquisite, and at times rare, photos of a wide variety of flora and fauna.

Her two books had remained on the New York Times best-seller list for weeks, and this trip's pictures would fill out the third book.

She often looked up to see that her fellow passengers were a good distance ahead after she had snapped her pics. Sybil had no fears while outdoors in wild country, once having stood as still as marble while snapping shots of a huge Kodiak bear in Alaska.

Her subtle reply to the local reporters that had heard about it was, "Looking into the view-finder I knew he was very close, and I could also smell his bad breath, but I just knew he wasn't going to hurt me, so I simply kept on snapping my pictures." Her tiny, dried-apple-doll face opened a wrinkled smile, "I truly believe he was enjoying the entire photo-shoot."

With her binoculars once again hanging around her tiny neck, Sybil lifted her right foot to begin closing the fifty-foot gap between her and Ozzie MacAnderson, a robust Scotsman who had worked his way back to the spot ahead of her.

Before that right boot ever touched the ground, a reticulated Burmese python that would later measure out at thirty-one-feet-three-inches, lunged up out of the dark water. By either design or accident, it had closed its sharp teeth in a huge open set of jaws, over her tiny mouth and nose. A second later, Sybil was under the water as the gigantic, prehistoric beast rolled three times and began using its muscular structure to squeeze every bit of air out of Sybil's lungs.

Not one of her fellow trail-walkers heard a thing, because as Sybil was being prepared for lunch, Jake was pointing out a very rare and beautiful wild orchid that is common in the Everglades.

A few minutes after Sybil had been pulled beneath the surface of the murky swamp, Ozzie MacAnderson looked back, expecting to see her rushing to catch up, as she often had done on the first leg of their walk.

All that a quick search located was her $1500 bouffant blonde wig lying on the trail. After running back down the trail as far as the wooden bridge, Jake bent over to catch his breath. He had built the bridge himself to go over the water, so that his walking-tour would have a completely different route back to the highway; Jake held to the bridge and gasped for air. Once he was breathing regularly again he walked slowly back to his waiting group, stopping every few feet to listen while scanning all of the surrounding bushes and growth along the edge of the river.

~ O ~

Mister Silver pulled on into the parking area of the spectacular

Ocean's 41 Goldmine Lounge and Gourmet Restaurant, which recently opened its doors in North Naples. Mister Gold silently scanned the entire area before he spoke. "I am quite pleased that this is the final meeting with Jerome. If Allah gives us his blessing, then everything should go exactly as we have planned."

"I have no doubts, Amad, that all will go as you wish. You have dreamed of this day for a very long time, and have worked hard to see that each and every detail has been attended to."

Amad nodded his head, "Yes, Jintan, five years on this one project has been taxing, but if it helps bring America to it's knees and runs them out of our country, then it will have been well worth the effort." He opened his door and stepped out.

"It's just my nature to be a bit skeptical," Jintan said during the walk toward the entrance, "with so much at stake, I usually feel at the last moment that something is going to wrong and we will be forced to start again."

Amad turned and said softly, "Remember, Jintan, you felt that way right up to the moment that our first plane crashed into the Twin Towers." He smiled as he opened the door, "It will go as smoothly as that operation, old friend. Come, let us see what Jerome has to say, and then we'll head back to the warehouse and see to it that everything is being done exactly as I ordered."

Amad told the maitre d'hotel that he had earlier reserved a private dining room. "And you are?" the stiff little man in the penguin tuxedo said as his waxed mustache wobbled like a rat's whiskers.

"Rutherford Burlington." Amad's dark eyes looked down at the nervous little penguin as though he was an annoying puppy.

"Ah yes," the penguin said as though the name rang a bell in his rodent head, "Mister Caldwell is waiting for you."

The penguin snapped his fingers, "Reiner, now!" The tall skeletal-thin young man left the tableful he was talking with and swished across the floor. "Yes, Renaldo."

"Escort Mister Burlington and his guest to room six."

Amad gave the penguin two twenty-dollar bills, and then said, "Thank you, Renaldo."

Reiner pulled back a section of the curtain of stringed shells and

Rick Magers

then followed the two dark men inside. After seating both men, he asked if they would like to order a drink before dinner.

"Yes," Amad replied, "two apricot brandy cocktails please and whatever Mister Caldwell would like."

Jerome said, "Bring me one of those, too."

"Very good, gentlemen, I shall be gone for only a tiny moment." The skeleton swished back through the curtain to get the drinks.

~ O ~

Outside the huge dinner house, the two CIA agents that had been following Amad and Jintan, double-parked just beyond the entrance and waited with the engine running. A minute later, the agent that had been ahead of them, also following the two terrorists, turned and walked back toward his automobile. He stopped briefly adjacent to the two agents in the car. He searched his pockets as though looking for something.

The agent driving lowered the window and listened as the agent searching his pockets said softly, "North wall, fifty feet from the front wall."

When the driver said, "Got it" the man pulled a set of keys from his pocket and turned as though he had found something that he thought he had left in his car, and then continued to the restaurant.

The two agents drove out and headed north on US 41. Only one minute later, a black SUV with tinted windows drove in and parked according to the instruction given to him over the cell phone by the two agents who had just pulled out.

The two agents sitting in front watched the area as the man in the rear used the very latest high-tech snooping microphone to scan the wall. Only moments after driving in, he said quietly, "I've got 'em, clear as a bell."

The lead agent said to himself, *like the Liberty Bell ringing at the execution of a few more terrorists.*

~ O ~

**R**onnie and Ziggy followed the trail they had come in on, until it dead-ended at a thick mass of swamp ferns and cypress trees. Ziggy said, looking back, "This trail we've got on must be another place they pulled a lot of logs out."

"You're right," Ronnie said as he looked at their back trail. "I didn't notice while we were walking, but now I can see that it zigzags back and forth more than those other ones back there do. Must be bigger logs in this area."

Ziggy walked past him and looked at the ferns. "Must always be wet right here, because I saw a guy on Animal Kingdom in a swamp somewhere pointing out ferns like these and it was all wet where they were." He shoved his red head into the ferns and then

Rick Magers

yelled, "Hey man, there's a big ole batch of eggs in here."

Before Ronnie could turn, Ziggy let loose a scream worthy of a role in a Hollywood Halloween horror film. Ronnie leaped back when he saw the size of the snake that had thrown two loops around his friend. He took two steps back as the blood drained from Ziggy's face. Ronnie's face turned chalk-white as he silently watched his friends face distorting like nothing in any of the many horror films he had watched with Ziggy.

All that was coming from Ziggy's mouth was a series of gasping wheezes as the twenty-foot long snake put on another loop, and then began squeezing his skinny body.

When Ronnie saw Ziggy's face turning as red as his hair he turned and ran. He thought he was running back down a trail made by him and Ziggy earlier, but he was actually in a two-foot-wide rut in the marshy area inside the hammock that was made by a huge python.

Though only an armchair TV show explorer, Ronnie had stumbled upon a mother-lode of reticulated pythons. In the next few months Abner Brown would increase his bank account considerably by ridding the hammock of fifty-three pythons and over nine hundred eggs that poor little Ronnie Weingarten and his pal and explorer, Ziggy, had inadvertently led him to.

~ O ~

Rick Magers

**B**y the time that Jake Brown finally reached the spot where Sybil

Schwat's wig was found lying along the edge of the path, and now there wasn't another sign of where she might be.

Ozzie MacAnderson was standing beside the blonde wig and mumbling repeatedly, "I looked back and she was gone, I looked back and.......uh......and.........."

Jake gave Ozzie a light pat on the shoulder, "It's not your fault Ozzie. Sybil was told, like everyone else, to stay one arm length from the person in front of them."

Ozzie dropped both arms and stood there shaking his head. "I stopped every time I saw her lagging back, so she could catch up with us. Oh man," he looked at the huge cypress tree near the blonde wig, "why did she stop here and let us get so far ahead on her?"

A short round woman with a butch haircut, wearing camo trousers and shirt, waddled toward Jake. Looking up at the side of the cypress tree she said, "Betcha she was taking some pictures of that," she pointed up at a wild orchid attached to a limb. "I saw it when we walked past, and thought, bet ole Siby takes a buncha pics of that one, because it's really a pretty orchid."

A tall slender woman wearing a designer sportsman suit nudged her way through the crowd. Looking up at the orchid she shook her head and almost groaned, "She sure spoiled our walking tour just to get a few pictures. Harrumph," she growled, "we have been seeing those all morning."

The little gal with the butch haircut punched her so hard in the stomach that she made a whooooosh sound and stumbled back. One of her designer boots caught on a tree root, and with her arms flailing like a scarecrow come to life, she fell backwards into the water.

"Oh my God," Jake yelled, and grabbed her reaching-out hand to help her climb back up on the path.

"You should have just let that snooty bitch drown," butch said, "she's been a pain in the ass all morning." She wheeled around, made her way through the crowd, and headed up the trail. "I reckon I'll see y'all at the bus." She glanced back to add, "That is if the snakes don't getcha."

Jake called 911 on his cell phone and explained what had happened, then asked the operator to connect him to the Sherriff's Sub Station at the Carnestown intersection of State Road 29 and Tamiami Trail.

When they answered, Jake said, "Jimmy, this is Jake Brown, and . . . . . he explained what had happened to Cybil but didn't mention a word about the brief wet scuffle between the two women. "Okay Jimmy, we'll be at my tour entrance on the bus by about eleven-thirty. I'll show the deputy that you send, where it happened while my tour people give the other deputy a required

Rick Magers

deposition."

"Come on folks," Jake said as cheerful and upbeat as he could, "let's finish the tour." A severely shaken and upset Jake Brown wormed his way on through the dour group and continued to point out the flora and fauna along the way back toward the bus.

They had no trouble hearing him. They were walking three abreast with those behind almost touching the ones ahead.

Jake Brown's mind was in a snarled turmoil as he trudged along. *This could be the end of my walking tour. If I survive this I'll do what Betty suggested; hire someone to walk at the end and keep 'em from lagging behind. Shit! Things were just beginning to look up.*

~ O ~

The three CIA agents who had just recorded the final meeting between Jerome and the two terrorists pulled out when they knew that this latest meeting was over. Two more agents were waiting outside to follow them.

When the first three agents were told that two other agents were following the conspiring terrorists, they headed straight toward Ft. Myers and pulled in, to park beneath the drab thirteen-story building an hour later.

Samson Blackraven listened as the tape was played back. The first voice he heard was Jerome Sennitt. 'Amad, this entire operation is finally coming together like a very well-rehearsed NFL football touchdown plan. Every man knows where he is supposed to be and what he must do.'

They rambled on for a while as they sipped their apricot brandy cocktails.

Samson tensed and leaned far forward. His nose was almost touching the speaker when he recognized Amad's voice.

~ O ~

Sixty miles northwest, Ronnie is now running for his life. His new jungle hat had been ripped from his head by a low hanging gumbo-limbo limb, leaving a severe gash. He was now bleeding profusely—always a lure for beasts of prey. The flimsy web-belt holding the tools of the new budding young adventurer was snatched from his waist as if a master pickpocket had taken a fancy to it and the toys hanging from it. The costly, new designer sunglasses went flying when Ronnie looked back and ran straight into a huge old cypress tree. Stunned by the blow, the boy rolled over on his hands and knees and watched as blood from his busted nose soon covered both of his small hands. Once his eyes had refocused, Ronnie saw a huge snake moving in his direction. Fear-powered, his skinny, twig-like legs performed miracles as they carried the screaming, bleeding boy through the swamp.

~ O ~

Sheenie walked along the side of the street that snaked along the

Barron River. When he got to Triad Seafood and Restaurant, he was

happy to see his old friend, Orlo Hilton, sitting in the small room

he used as an office and bullshit parlor when friends dropped in.

"Is Julie chewin on your ass again?" Orlo smiled and slid open

the bottom left drawer.

While Orlo scooped some ice cubes into both highball glasses

from the Igloo in the corner, Sheenie settled into the small lumpy

couch and said, "You mean t'say there was a time that you can

remember when that old hack wasn't?" He took the glass and

drained half of the amber liquid.

"Hmmmm," Orlo sorta crooned, "naaaaah, seems like she has

been bumping her gums at you for about as long as I've known

her." He tilted his glass but only sliced off a small shot.

"Forty-five goddamned years, for me."

"That long huh? Damn, time flies when yer havin fun, huh?"

Orlo's grin was subtle, but his ever-mischievous eyes twinkled.

Sheenie twirled the ice and scotch around and was silent for a

moment. "Woulda been a helluva lot more fun if I hadn't let her get

on the damn boat that day I headed across the bay to here from

Marathon."

Rick Magers

"What's it about this time?"

"That witch, Phyliss MacAllenby. Julie agrees with an old crone like that because she agrees that the airboats are too loud." He drained the glass and held it out for a refill.

Orlo shook his head. "Damned snowbuzzards come down here from a place where everything is loud, blowin their horns, and big jets flying in all hours day n' night. Goddamn traffic is so loud y'can't hear yerself think, and every boob tube is set on full-throttle because they are all deaf. Then they want all the airboats quieted down with them damn five thousand dollar mufflers." Orlo shook his head again and drained his own glass.

"Gotta accept it I reckon," Sheenie moaned, "from a bunch of ignoramus people that spent all of their good years where it snows so hard the Mounties gotta dig 'em out before they freeze solid."

Orlo's soft sarcastic laugh jingled. Finally he said, "I forgot, Phyllis and Cord are Canadian." He chuckled a bit longer while filling their glasses again.

"They still bring those goddamned barking poodles of theirs when they come here to eat now n' then?"

"Well, not in the last couple of years," Orlo smiled, "they haven't. My waitresses stopped serving the tight bastards. They all got sick n' tired of picking up fresh poodle shit around the table after they left. Those damn Canadians seldom tip, and when they do it's usually just pennies."

Rick Magers

"Yassuh," Sheenie agreed, "those cheap assholes ain't welcome anyplace that I know of any more." Sheenie sipped on his scotch, "Everyone usta say that Jews were cheap, but that's bullshit. Most Jews tip good for service and quality food. A good waitress won't work in a Jewish place that serves shitty steaks, or doesn't change the oil in the fryolators, and stuff like that. If a waitress or a waiter brings a Jew a lousy steak, it's their own damn fault they don't get good tips, because a smart one will take it back to the cook and tell him to shove it up his ass and then cook her one right, just like they ordered. But with Canadians it doesn't help the ole tip jar to give 'em good service and bring superb food that's cooked perfectly, the bastards are just tightwads, as any bartender or waiter will tell you."

Sheenie drained his glass and handed it to Orlo. "Gonna walk up the road n' see if Delvin Watson's got that hydraulic trap puller on his trap boat fixed yet." He slowly stood and then twisted around a bit to limber up. "Thanks for the ear and booze, Orlo. I feel a bit better now just talking to somebody with brains between their ears."

"Don't be too hard on her Sheenie," Orlo grinned, "you'll be missin her once she's in the ground."

"Yeah, sure." Sheenie grumbled as he stepped off the concrete, "Like I'll miss these damn hemhorroids."

Orlo leaned against the doorjam and watched the old man as he

Rick Magers

hobble toward the area where several commercial boats were tied to pilings. *Tough ole bugger in his day. I'm gittin old m'self, and it sure ain't som'n t'look forward to, specially with a cranky old woman chewin on your ear all the time.*

~ O ~

**A**bner Brown had just dropped Engelburt off at the stilthouse that he rented from Lynn McMillin. "I'll give you a call when I've got everything ready to go out on the Swamp Castle. Probably be Thursday." He waved and pulled away.

*Boy*, Engelburt thought as he trudged up the stairs, *I can't wait to see that rig. Seeing how he does everything, it'll probably be in tip-top shape.* At the top of the steps he got on the porch and leaned back against the rail as he tried to retrieved the breath he had lost halfway up. *Gotta get m'self a bicycle and start getting back in shape.*

Once inside he grabbed a beer and began shedding clothes as he moved toward the bathroom. He sat the half full beer on the toilet reservoir, stepped out of his Fruit of the Looms, and stood beneath the cold water for a full five minutes. *I think I could hear my brain frying while we were on that airboat. Hope I didn't lose too many brain cells cause I didn't have many spares to start with.*

With a second cold beer beside him he sat in his fresh shorts as he began updating everything on his laptop. After reading what he

Rick Magers

had just entered, he leaned back and stretched.

"Okay, okay, okay." He looked down at his growling stomach, "I think a trip to Billy Potters oughta shut you up. One more growl though and we'll stay here n' finish the Mac n' Cheese."

Just as he closed the door and started down the steps, the loudest stomach growl he'd ever had erupted. "Knew I was just bullshittin, huh?" Another growl as he climbed in the car brought a smile to his face. "I wonder if they have any of that yummy Ramen Noodle Soup left?" A barbed pain was accompanied by a loud growl. *It's gonna be rough if I ever get stranded on an island without food for a day or two. That stomach'll start eating me.*

Engelburt glanced at the young girl walking on the bicycle path toward Everglades City. A moment later he pulled over and stopped. Getting out, he moved to the rear and waved at her, "Hey, Maggie, we met the other day, remember? It was when Abner Brown and I stopped in for a beer. Need a ride or are you walking for a little exercise?"

She walked toward him with a big smile making her pretty face even more attractive. "Engelburt, right?"

"Yep! Good memory."

"Gotta have one t'be a good bartender or waitress, and no, I'm not walking for exercise, and yes, I need a ride to work."

"Hop in," he smiled wide, "we were just on our way to the Seafood Depot."

Rick Magers

Maggie snapped off her seat belt and twisted to look at the area behind the two bucket seats, "We?"

She loved his spontaneous laugh. "My stomach has been a growling companion all afternoon."

"Mine does the same thing if I wait too long to shove something down my neck for it to snack on." She leaned her head of thick red hair out the window a bit then turned toward him. "What kind of mufflers y'got on this thing? Quietest car I've ever been in."

"Ab said the same thing. No mufflers, it's electric." He turned toward her and flashed his ivory white tooth smile.

When Maggie looked over and saw his dimples, her stomach did a slight tug and she had to wait a moment to get her breath controlled again to speak. "Seen em on TV, Ford Thunder Eagle, Right?"

"Yep, my college friend and editor of the magazine I work for, bought it for me when he recently inherited some dough."

"Those kind of pals are few and far between. Must be nice driving right past the gas pump since it went up to over eleven bucks a gallon for regular."

"Sure is, that why you're walking? Traded yours in for a new pair of Nike Flyers?" He turned and grinned at her again, which caused her stomach to flip again.

"Nah, then I'd hafta keep a second wardrobe at the restaurant, walking in this kind of heat. A friend drove it to Naples for me to

Rick Magers

have new tires put on. Her daddy has a tire store, and this week he is offering one tire free if you'll buy three, plus the balancing and installation is included."

"Can't beat that if the three are reasonable."

"Little over seven hundred."

"That's a good deal." He pulled in and parked close to the entrance. At the door he asked, "Can I have dinner at the bar?"

"Sure, c'mon in, and I'll find out what's really fresh if you plan on having fish."

"That's about all I have eaten since I got here. I watched Orlo one day over at his restaurant, Triad, and he was busy cleaning the fish that he was serving that day."

"He's an old-timer around here, and does everything like they used to, when this was just a small fishing village. My best girl friend works there as a waitress and she says that Orlo and Pam are both real sticklers about a plate of their food being fresh and cooked right."

"I like 'em both alot," Engelburt said as he pulled the front door open, "he's funny as hell at times."

On the way to the patio she turned her head back, "Get him to tell you some of his stories about," She put her eyebrows way up and wobbled them, "the good ole days back in the 70s."

"I will."

"Grab a stool and tell Ellie what you wanna drink, and I'll get my register set up so she can leave, then I'll get your food order."

An hour later, Engelburt had finished a huge plate of fried fish, cole slaw, home-made french fries, and four hushpuppies. He had been watching while Maggie made drinks for all of the dining room waitresses, and moving effortlessly back and forth serving the full bar in the chickee where he sat.

He watched as she swiftly scooted out of the bar and disappeared down through the diners in the main dining room. *Musta had to pee bad*, he thought and swiveled left to watch one of the tour airboats coming back in from a trip across the Everglades.

"Here you go, Burt, this is on me for the ride." She placed a huge slice of Key Lime Pie on the bar.

After swiveling back around he said, "You're psychic too, huh, Maggie?"

"Why, thatcher favorite?"

"Since I was about ten, when we took our first Florida vacation."

"Where was home back then?"

"Boston, ever been there?"

"Nope."

"Don't go. I use to think it was a great place to live until I came to Miami in 2010 to attend college."

"Holy mackerel," Maggie's wide white smile flashed and Engelbert felt a huge sunami wave rush through his stomach, "we

Rick Magers

probably went past each other in the halls many times. I was there from 2010 until I graduated and got my degree in 2014. Small world, huh?"

"Yeah, it is until you see how many students are in each of the hundreds of classes these days." He smiled, flashing his perfect white-as-pearls teeth, and Maggie's heart beat fast for a moment, something that very seldom happened. "We might have been in the same class at times and never met."

She turned when her name was called. "Okay Jimmy, you want another Coors, right?" She got a fresh bottle from the beer cooler and carried it to an old man that always seemed to be sitting at the same place every time Engelburt had visited the chickee bar."

Between orders Maggie and Engelburt chatted about their days at the University of Miami and a variety of other topics, just to keep them near each other. By closing time it was very obvious to each of them that there was something quite special that was beginning to develop between the two of them.

"Maggie," Engelburt said quietly when she began wiping the bar near him, and getting everything placed correctly for the following day, "I'll be happy to give you a ride home if you haven't already made arrangements."

"That's great, Burt, thanks. I was just gonna call my roommate and ask her to please pick me up." Her warm  sincere smile sent a shiver up his spine, "Thanks very much. I know she's snuggled up in bed watching TV."

Half an hour later he had dropped her off at a small house on Chokoloskee and was beneath the stilt house plugging the car into his charger to top off the batteries.

~ O ~

Christina Shalah Galindo was walking along the side of the street with her young daughter, Angelina. They had arrived direct from Guademala, right at the beginning of summer and they now live permanently in Everglades City. Christina's husband, Eduarto Jose Galindo, had drowned while working as a diver on a salvage vessel owned by an American, but was registered in Honduras.

Christina was born in Limon, Honduras and had never been farther away than Puerto Castilla. Christina was fifteen when she met Eduarto at a Sunday picnic that was sponsored by her church.

Eduarto was born in Puerto Quetzal, Guademala and was, like Christina, also a Baptist. He was thrilled when the pastor invited him to their annual, meet-a-new-friend picnic. He'd only been working on the salvage vessel a few months and, being the most recent hired, Eduarto was expected to remain on the vessel as long as it was on the anchor, and resting above the Spanish galleon. They were only about ten miles from Limon, Honduras, and the ships' motor-launch was lowered from the deck by one of the cranes every weekend, so the ships' main crewmembers that had been aboard for several years could visit their girlfriends. Eduarto, one of the cooks, and one of the two captains always watched the launch heading in toward shore with longing hearts.

None more so than Eduarto. He had learned to use a scuba tank and diving gear, and later was certified by a Master/Diver-Instructor. Eduarto loved the work he was doing, but his twenty year old eyes filled with tears each time he came out on deck at night and saw the glowing lights of Limon.

The church picnic was a very successful event each year. Most of the protestants showed up faithfully to enjoy the dividends of their weekly donations.

Eduarto was thrilled to be allowed off of the salvage vessel until Monday morning. The pastor had taken an immediate liking to the young Honduran the previous year when the boat that Eduarto was working on, docked at the city wharf. When the crew all went to the local bar, Eduarto walked up to the old pastor and spoke. "I see by your dress that you are a priest, father. Am I correct?"

"Yes, my son, I am the Baptist pastor of Limon. Can I help you?"

"Yes, father, I am also a Baptist and would like to attend church on the days that I have off. Can you tell me where your church is and what days it is open?"

Rick Magers

The old pastor smiled, "Go to the edge of town," he pointed south, "and you will see the tall steeple when you look left toward the east. It's not as far as it appears and is a very peaceful walk. Flowers bloom all along the road, all year round." His grin now had a mischievous twinkle when he reached inside his tattered old jackets' pocket. Holding a card, he said, "Here is my card. I live in the house behind with my wife and two sons. Turn it over and you will see that it states 'I am here to help you seven days a week, twenty-four hours a day.'

The old man smiled and gently patted Eduarto on the shoulder, "Whenever you have time away from work, please come and visit with us as though we are your home and family away from home."

After almost one year on the Salvage Vessel, Rainbow's End, Eduarto was considered to be permanent crew. Four divers were fired for drinking on board the ship, and one young diver was frightened by a huge tigershark. The youth quit as soon as he got back on deck.

Eduarto had been confronted by sharks twice, and each time, he had kept his composure until the sharks closed in, and then he hit one in the gills with his Shock-Stick. After a good bolt of electricity surged through the shark's system, it was then immediately ready to look elsewhere for a bite to eat.

Rick Magers

Instances such as that, and the fact that Eduarto was always a ready to help man with whatever task was tackled by the crew, and the fact that he never complained, made him a well-liked member.

On one trip to Limon, Pastor Julio Eglesias Montania introduced Eduarto to thirteen year old Christina Shalah Solana. Later on he would tell the pastor that it was the best day of his life.

They were married four months later. Ten months after that, Angelina Maria Galindo was born. The pastor located a very small house for them to rent. Each time Eduarto was given a full weekend off he hurried straight home to spend every moment with his new family. It was actually the only true home he ever had. Like Christina, Eduarto had also become an orphan at a very young age. While spending the night at his best friend's home across town, his parents and younger brother died when their house caught fire in the middle of the night.

Three year old Eduarto Jose Galindo was placed in a Baptist-sponsored orphanage in the small town of Puerto Barrios, Guatamala.

The pleasure of finally having his very own family was a short lived afair. Three months after Angelina was born, her daddy, Eduarto was killed. He was following a 17th century bronze cannon that was being raised from the Spanish galleon they were diving on. Twenty feet above the galleon the cable winch aboard the salvage vessel, a hundred feet above, suddenly slipped out of gear.

Rick Magers

Eduarto's dive partner later said that one moment the canon was going up just fine, and the next thing he saw from but fifty feet away, was Eduarto being crushed beneath the huge canon against the ballast pile.

~ O ~

**R**onnie Weingarten had somehow made it through the swamp, and was now running on a narrow path. Five minutes later he was standing on a shell mound looking around. *Can this be the same mound we were on a while ago?* His thoughts were scrambled as he turned around to see if any of the huge snakes had followed him. *Where is Ziggy? Oh God, Ziggy's dead. Which way is the airboat? Where's my hat?* He reached down and searched his waist. *Where is my canteen? My jungle knife is gone, too.* He pulled a hankerchief from his pocket and blew his nose. *Ow, ow, my darn nose must be busted.* He watched as blood ran freely and began covering the shells and twigs. *How did I break my nose? Did we crash the airboat? Did Ziggy hit me on the nose? Why didn't he come with me?* He simply wilted down to the shell mound and sat there mumbling with his head facing the ground. He heard a noise behind him so he stood and wobbled toward a huge gumbo limbo tree. It had limbs sticking out low enough that he could reach one to help him get up into it. He climbed until he was up where the limbs were getting a

Bit small, so he settled into a junction of three limbs.

As the sun began going down, he remembered something he had once seen on a television show. He pulled his belt out of the loops and after getting as comfortable as possible, Ronnie used it to fasten his leg to the limb it was resting on. *That guy in the jungle,* he thought, *would have fallen into the quicksand once he fell asleep if he had not tied his leg to the tree.*

When he was finally tied securely in, and had settled down, he turned and looked down to see if he could find what had made the noise, earlier. Slowly and painfully, he turned his head as far as it would go in each direction to see what it was.

Just before dark Ronnie spotted a movement among the leaves a few feet from the tree. His mind slipped into panic-mode. *I wonder if pythons can climb trees. I wish I still had my survival knife. Maybe I could…maybe I could…if I just had…shit, there's not a thing I can do.* He leaned back against the trunk and closed his eyes. Several minutes later he opened his eyes and watched the last of the sunshine slowly turn his world into a black nightmare.

He began to silently pray. *Dear God, please help me. I'm not really a bad person, even though I've done some stupid things…*he paused…*like this, but I have never hurt anyone on purpose, and I've always been good to dogs and other animals, and I'm really sorry I switched that ten mama gave me for a dollar bill that time in church, and Lord…*his prayers continued through the night, and were still coming when the sun

Rick Magers

began lighting his world once again.

~ O ~

Amad's voice was clear and distinct. As he listened, Sampson Blackraven's eyes narrowed. When he leaned forward his eyes resembled those of a man about to pull the trigger.

"We will teach those infidels that they cannot invade our country and change our religion and way of life. If this message does not tell them that they must leave our country and never return, then we will continue our mission until there is nothing left of America to rebuild."

"Yes," Samson heard Jerome Sennitt agree, "I too am fed up with the methods that America is using to gain control of all the countries that do not bow down to the rules they create. As soon as this operation is over, I'm my moving entire family back to Cuba."

"You were a Marine Embassy Guard in Cuba," Amad said, "when you met your wife, correct?"

"Yes. I was a young man and did not understand how America was trying to gain control of the entire world. Once we complete this mission, I plan to make a new start in life, back to Cuba. Capitalism is already warping my young daughter and son."

Samson ground his teeth together when Amad spoke. "With the family of your wife in Cuba, and the powerful contacts that I have in Cuba, you will do quite well."

Samson could almost see Amad smile. "And you will no longer have to deal with these spoiled rotten Hypocrites who run this evil capitalist country." Samson's dark eyes narrowed as he imagined the two terrorists, Amad and Jintan, eating the extravagant food that their poor countrymen would never taste. *And, you disgusting sonuvabitch,* Samson thought, *you have the audacity to call us a bunch of spoiled Hypocrites.*

Samson's spy continued, "Yes, I am fed up with these thieving politicians who pick our pocket clean with one hand and pat us on the back with the other."

"With the five blows that we are about to deliver to America, all of those days will be gone. While the first city is still suffering from the blow, we will unleash a second, and later a third, fourth, and fifth. And if that does not bring them to their knees, then the final blow, one that is being prepared as we speak, will be a biological nightmare from which very few Americans will survive."

Something that Samson could not possibly see was Jerome's smile when he lifted his glass slightly as a toast, but was thinking, *how in the hell did I ever get involved with these two crazy goddamn Muslim terrorists?* When Jintan leaned forward with his glass in hand, Jerome saw that Amad had a second wolf at his side.

Their dinners arrived, so the conversation stopped as they ate a meal that few people in Iran would ever be financially able to enjoy. Samson was fortunate not to be able to see the two terrorists

Rick Magers

eating and drinking in the country they were planning to destroy.

Samson Blackraven's dark eyes were emotionally glued onto the recorder, as he replayed a portion. When he heard Amad say, "And if that does not bring them to their knees, then the final blow; one that is being prepared as we speak, will be a biological nightmare from which very few Americans will survive." Samson punched a number that brought the Director of the National Security Agency to his video screen in a few short moments.

Haleole Hokulani became the Director of the N S A when he retired as a bird colonel in the Navy SEAL organization. He was born in Honolulu, Hawaii, into a family of seventh generation Hawaiians that combined their pride as native Hawaiians with the pride they felt as American citizens.

"What's up, Chief?"

Samson answered, "I just received some new and frightening developments in Operation Swamprat, Hal."

"Hang on a sec, Chief."

Samson knew exactly what he was doing, so when The Director returned to say, "Wanted to be certain that we're on triple X red. Shoot, Chief cause ain't nobody here but us and the recorder." Samson smiled wide knowing that the line they were speaking on was secure.

"Big upgrade, Hal, listen to this." Samson plugged in the very latest recording of Jerome and his two Iranian terrorists.

~ O ~

**B**urt was up and dressed early. Just as he had finished a eating a fried egg sandwich and a bowl of Wheaties, he heard Abner's big muffler roar while gearing down as he came through the pines into Viking Country. He grabbed his camera and recorder and met Abner as he pulled up. "Got everything done, eh?"

"Yeah," Abner drawled, "there wasn't too much t'do, and for a change everything went good."

"That leaking gearbox on your swamp castle wasn't a big deal, then?"

"Just needed a new gasket and the diesel generator only needed a new fuel cartridge. She's now running great and not sputtering and spitting." As he pulled away he looked over, "Burt, y'wanna stop n' get breakfast?"

"You're drivin, man, you find a place n' I'll buy."

"You always this goddamn hard t'git along with?"

"Started my period this morning."

Ab laughed and whipped left into the Havana Café beside the Chokoloskee Post Office.

Two huge plates of home fries, eggs, sausage, and toast later, the two men stood. Ab said, "Gonna check my mail while you pay, and by the way, I left the tip on the table."

Rick Magers

After paying the bill, Burt stepped outside and smiled wide as Maggie pulled in. She stepped out of her car grinning, "Hiya Burt, I reckon you're goin out with Ab today, huh?"

"Yep," he answered as his eyebrows furrowed a bit, "news moves faster here than in Miami."

Abner had come out of the post office, and before she could answer, he said, "Maggie and Ginger," he nodded at the girl standing beside Maggie, "my girlfriend are house mates and I stopped by to see if they needed a ride to work."

Burt groaned as Abner headed toward Everglades City, "I can't believe I shoved that breakfast in on top of the egg sandwich and a bowl of Wheaties I ate just before you pulled in."

"You oughta," Abner said, "be able to get a good deal when you trade that snazzy little Ford in on som'n with a door big enough for you to get in."

Burt turned to look at a grinning Abner, "I might ask you to let me out when you turn onto your road, so I can walk in."

"I might not eat dinner tonight either, Burt."

"Uh huh, right."

~ O ~

Gregory Watson, Delvin's younger brother, known to locals as Relapse, was holding a rusty old pistol that was pointed straight at

Morton Gomez. "It's settling the score time, damn you," he literally screamed, "for killin my great-great grandpa, Edgar Watson, you no good forin, spic, sonuvbitch." He kept opening and closing his mouth like a barracuda; big difference since there were only a few black rotted stumps left in his mouth.

Everyone in the two small towns and Plantation Key knew that Gregory was a walking scarecrow cadaver, and was being controlled and motivated by brain mush that was melted on crank and crack a decade earlier. A few that had been confronted by him, knew that he certainly was not just a harmless druggie that was just tread-milling his way toward the graveyard.

It was the 4th of July 2020 at the annual Independence Day picnic in Everglades City. He had driven up to the outdoor picnic in a 1943 Army Jeep. Nobody was ever able to learn where he got things like the Jeep. At a very young age, his natural talent about mechanical objects, from a simple home toaster to an automobile, became apparent. He could fix anything that needed fixing and get any engine running that wasn't. Some thought he was Idiot Savant. Most said that he was just an idiot who knew how to fix things.

His brother Delvin, older by three years, knew as a young boy that brother Greg was not mentally up to par. Gregory's father, Otto, knew it was true and knew why, as did Lulu Watson, Greg's older sister — who was also, unknown to even Gregory, his mother.

Morton Gomez was shivering as though he was stuck outside in a snowstorm. His milky eyes were locked onto the huge black hole in the end of Gregory's rusty old pistol.

Greg was rapidly tiring. The rusty old relic weapon was slowly lowering. He would notice it and jerk it back up so it was pointing straight at Morton. Each time he did, his pointed chin would be thrust out and he would begin rotating his head back and forth in a circle.

The third time that Greg did that neck-rotating thing, his big brother Delvin used a two-by-four he'd found leaning against a clothes line, to knock the pistol out of Greg's hand.

"Ow, owwww, ooooooooow, Greg screamed and went down to his knees. When his brother moved around in front of him to stand leaning on the twisted two-by-four, Greg looked up with tears flooding his eyes. "Why did you hit me, Delvin?"

"To keep you from going into the execution chamber, up in Raiford Prison, where daddy now lives."

Greg wiped away the tears with his shirtsleeve and screamed, "Thet goddamm Morton kilt our own kinfolk, Delvin." His black-stump filled mouth began opening and closing as he rotated his odd-shaped head.

"C'mon, bro," Delvin said, "we gotta get on out there n' set that load of crab traps before dark." He reached down and grabbed the left hand that was holding up the swollen right hand. Greg's left had only a thumb and pinkie so he often used it as a fork to hold the end of a board, drain gutter, etc. After being gone a month when he was fifteen, he arrived back home with the modified hand. He swore he had no memory of how or why he lost the three fingers.

Even at sixteen, his brother, Delvin, was a very savvy young guy. He once told his father, "Greg's been hanging around with a bad bunch of drug dealers in Naples, and he probably screwed 'em. I bet they sliced off his fingers as a warning to him and anyone else that thought they could cheat the gang."

"Yeah Del," his father had slurred, "that kid ain't never had a lick o' sense and warnt a bit o' meat between his ears."

"Ow, ow, ow," Greg wailed as he struggled to his feet and followed his brother to the truck.

Fifteen minutes later, they were moving south on the Barron River and heading toward the bay, and then on out into the Gulf of Mexico. Delvin's 49 foot boat was loaded with stone crab traps.

Greg was lying in one of the two narrow bunks in the wheelhouse. He was holding his swollen hand up with the other fork-hand, and moaning softly.

Delvin stood at the wheel shaking his head. Dark thoughts ran through his brain. *I can't keep this shit up any longer. Daddy's doin life up in Raiford n' mama's in the nursing home to stay now. Greg's gonna kill somebody one of these days, sure as shit stinks.* He looked back at his brother lying there holding the swollen hand up. Shaking his head, Delvin thought, *probably throbs when he doesn't hold it up.* Tears came to his eyes, so he turned back and continued looking out through the windshield. *If he kills somebody, the damn court's gonna ask why I didn't have him committed someplace where he could be looked after.* He closed his eyes shut tight for a moment. *That would be a Hell that even he doesn't deserve.*

~ O ~

Chuck Daggolonie had been talking to the four young Marco Island adventure seekers for a couple of hours. He had just scored a vial of good liquid crank, and went into the men's room of the Golden Goose, a watering hole on north Tamaimi Trail. After putting a few drops on his pre-rolled joints of sinsemilla he returned to the table. "Hey kids," he said quietly, even though he was only about twenty-five and they were all in their late teen years, "let's blow this place and go outside and burn a doobie."

All had smoked marijuana, but among them none had ever smoked a joint soaked with speed. By the time the second soaked joint was passed around and ended up as a snack between Chuck's teeth, all four of the *kids* were stoned like never before.

Chuck had watched then with a grin hiding his greed.

"Man," Alan Prescott, the nineteen year old heir to the Prescott Law Firm in the Big Apple, and now Marco Island, said, "that is the best damn joint I've ever shoved between my lips."

Arlene Scheel, Alan's first girlfriend, at seventeen had not only smoked marijuana a few times, but she agreed with Alan.

Joel Levis, at eighteen years old, had probably already smoked more marijuana than any of his friends, but he had never smoked a joint soaked with speed. "That ain't west coast reefer, man," he smiled at Chuck, "but it's sure better'n the shit I been getting around here."

Joel's girlfriend for the past year, sixteen year old Belinda Yevitz threw her hands in the air. "Dude, your joint ain't the best thing I ever had shoved between my lips," she looked at Joel and wobbled her eyebrows, "but that is really some good shit." She grinned wide, "Makes me wanna get naked and screw."

Alan turned toward Chuck, "Got some of that good shit for sale, dude?"

"I have five joints in this mint tin," he lifted it out of his shirt pocket, and then let it drop back down.

Alan leaned toward him and almost fell off the picnic table. After recovering his balance he asked Chuck if he'd sell all five.

"Sure, man, they're twenty bucks each."

Without hesitation Alan peeled off five twenties from a roll of bills. After he handed him the money and had shoved the mint tin back down into his pocket, he asked, "Gonna have s'more soon?"

"Sure man, how about right here day after tommorow about eight in the evening?"

Rick Magers

"We will be here," Alan looked over at his three friends, "right, guys 'n' gals?" They all agreed.

Two days later at 8 o'clock, all four of them were sitting at a corner table in the dark end of the room. The Golden Goose Restaurant and Lounge was well known to all of the local druggies and dealers as a good place to operate from.

The lounge was huge, so it was usually easy to get a table away from everyone, and it was also kept very dark inside.

As long as Tango Rumelli, the owner, was handed a small bag containing a little of whatever the dealer was pushing, plus a nice slice of the proceeds, all was okay. Tango's house rules were few but solid as granite and no second chances: no using inside of his establishment, no fights, arguments, or loud talking. During the three years that Chuck Daggolonie had been using this place as his headquarters, he had seen only one guy break the rules.

A young kid from New Jersey brought five kilos of cocaine to test the waters, so-to-speak. He sold the entire five kilos in a week—the dope was that good. The young preppie druggies kept coming back to the Golden Goose with a wad of daddy's dough.

This Jersey guy, Pingo or Peego, none of the regulars ever figured out which, Bretski, was raking in dough but never gave Tango his cut.

When Tango confronted Dingo, that was a nickname we hung on the little squirt, this kid went off in a very loud and nasty way.

Tango just quietly said, "I will get with you later, do not upset the customers, please."

Dingo strutted around like one of my old granny's bantam roosters the rest of the night. "Taught that wop a goddamn lesson," he said several times.

The kid, Dingo, never showed up at the Golden Goose again — or anyplace else I reckon. A guy from Jersey came down asking about him. Tango invited the guy into his office up on the second floor. He must have explained everything to him, because he left that same day. Never heard a thing about Dingo after that.

A few days later, the same two boys and two girls were sitting outside under one of the three palmetto-thatched chickees that Tango had a Seminole Indian friend build when the restaurant and lounge was completed.

Chuck Daggolonie pulled in towing his airboat. He parked and walked over with a wide smile. "Hey, y'all wanna go out in the Everglades for a while and chase the gators?"

All four of them were bored, and jumped at the opportunity to do something different for a change.

They all piled into his four-door pickup truck and hit the road toward a friend's place in East Naples where they could launch the airboat.

One hour after they had climbed into his truck, the five of them were roaring across the Everglades.

"Man," Alan said, "this is one nice airboat, dude."

"Quietest one I've ever been in," Arleen commented.

Chuck turned toward her, "Took five grand worth of mufflers to quiet it down. I don't like having those damn Park Rangers knowing where I am. When they shut down I throttle back, and wait'll they fire back up. That way," he grinned at them, "I know where they are but they don't have a clue where I'm running."

It was almost dark when Chuck eased back on the throttle. The prop turned slowly as the Engine idled. He turned toward Belinda, "Have you ever seen a python up close?"

"What's a python?" She had just taken a huge toke and her pupils looked like tiny black dots. She handed the joint to her boyfriend, Joel.

Joel took a long deep pull before passing the joint to Alan. "It's a big ass snake," he said grinning at Belinda.

"Well shit," Arleen giggled, "let's go catch the fucker and I'll take it to school with me."

The joint returned to Chuck too small for him to get a last toke, so he ate it. "Okay girls n' boys, let's go find a python."

Joel almost fell out of the boat when Chuck put the pedal to the metal. Belinda fell on Arleen's lap and Alan squated with one hand on the gunwale with the other gripping the rail on the back of the seat.

~ All were laughing as the boat flew across the sawgrass ~

**A**fter thirty minutes of pedal-to-the-metal running across the Everglades—the airboat's headlights abruptly went out. Instead of slowing down to see what the problem was, Chuck kept his foot on the pedal shoving down. In his stoned mind, or what was left of it, after years of speed constantly altering its programming, he might have been seeing the sky as a brilliantly illuminated panarama that was guiding him to a beach called paradise where he could jockey the airboat to a graceful landing.

## ~ IT DIDN'T HAPPEN THAT WAY ~

~ O ~

**A**bner stopped to pick up Burt an hour before sunrise. "I see you brought a lunch," he said, "at least it looks like a lunch bag."

Burt lifted the small brown bag, "Four peanut butter, banana, and strawberry jam sandwiches."

"Hotdamn," Ab said with a grin that Burt couldn't see in the dark truck, "thanks for thinking of me. Shoulda brought yourself four too."

"I'm on a diet, plus I try to keep on the good side of anyone that I see carrying a gun as big as yours. I'm from Miami, y'know."

Rick Magers

"That was my small one, wait'll you see what I carry on the Swamp Castle."

"Does it take two men to hold it?"

"Nah, I can hold it on my shoulder and all you gotta do is shove the missile in and tap me on the head."

"Oh shit."

Abner smiled in the darknesss.

When they crossed Tamiami Trail and kept on driving north, Burt said, "This's twenty-nine that goes up to Sebring, isn't it?"

"Yeah, been up this way before, huh?"

"Once, quite a while back, I rode along with a friend, just to watch the race."

"Always wanted to do that," Abner said, "but never got around to it."

After a while, Burt asked, "Do you keep your swamp buggy at someone's place out here?"

"Nope, I've got forty acres with a ninety-nine year lease out here right next to the Everglades."

"Wow, y'musta put that hogleg to good use."

Abner chuckled, "Nah, daddy had made some very good friends in state and federal government. The lease is good as long as one of his direct decendants lives on it."

"You have a house out here too, huh?"

"Wayeeeeell," Ab drawled the word out, "uhhh, sorta."

Burt just chuckled softly and leaned his head back and snoozed. He had spent the night at the Seafood Junction, watching Maggie fix drinks for the chickee bar's patrons. When she was finally finished setting the bar up for the next day's bartender, Burt drove her home. They sat in his car chatting for an hour before she yawned and told him she was dead tired.

She pressed the door button while saying, "You stay seated, I'll come around." When she got to his open window she leaned in and gave him a toe-curling kiss. "I really like you, Burt."

After catching his breath he said, "G'nite, Maggie. I like you too." He paused a moment then added, "A lot."

After putting her key in the front door lock she turned, and with a smile that made his stomach twist, said, "I'm glad you do." With a wave she went inside."

~ O ~

"Okay man," Abner said, with a jingle in his voice. "Time to make the donuts. Sun's up and snakes are waitin' for us." Burt sat up wiping the sleep out of his eyes. "Stayed up too damn late again, I guess. Wish there was a Dunkin Donuts place right here. How long did I snooze?"

"About half an hour. I can make a pot of coffee, if that's whacha need." Abner had stopped the truck in front of a very huge metal

Quonset hut. "Home sweet home," he crooned, and then climbed out of the truck and headed toward a steel door with Burt right behind him. "It won't be Dunkin Donuts type coffee, but it'll wake you up."

"Wasn't coffee I was thinkin about, it was those great diet pancakes that they make." Abner chuckled. Burt added, "I was just kidding about a stack of diet pancakes, I'm a growing young feller, y'know." That got a laugh.

When they stepped inside, Burt just stood there, his mouth hanging a bit open. "Holy shit, man, is that the Swamp Castle or a mobile cabin you rent to tourists?"

"That's her."

"Got an elevator to get up in it?"

"Nah, just a coupla steps and you're on the second floor."

"What's on the first floor?" Burt looked at Abner like maybe he was kidding.

"That's the freezer room. It's five feet deep with the hatches on the floor of the main room where I've got a stove and a good microwave to cook with and a fridge t'keep the food in. Two bunks fold up against the walls and there's a small air conditioner, so we don't hafta deal with mosquitos or those goddamned saber-tooth gnats that come out at dawn n' dusk."

"Eeeyowww," Burt squeeled, "I didn't know what the hell was eating me until Maggie told me about those no-see-ums. That must be what you call saber-tooth gnats. She also told me to get a bottle of Avon Skin-so-Soft at the Marathon station in Everglades City."

"Yeah, the manager's wife is the local Avon lady, and it really does keep those bastards from ruining your day. C'mon Burt, lemme show you my Swamp Castle."

Burt followed Abner as he flipped switches that lit up the fifty by one hundred foot Quanset hut that was forty feet high at the center. When they arrived beside the swamp buggy Burt stopped beside one of the four rear tires. "Damn, these tires are taller than I am, and I'm six feet tall."

"Yeah they are," Ab answered, "and they can take me damn near anywhere out here I'd wanna go." He grinned at Burt, "But I sure hope they last until we get these snakes oughta here."

"Costly, ain't they?"

"Twenty-two hundred apiece."

"Ouch."

"Well," Ab drawled, "they keep me up high so I can see everything I need to, and if everything concerning these pythons goes as planned, they'll end up being a good investment." Abner made a motion with his hand, "C'mere n' have a look under her."

Engelburt followed him to the rear, and then he looked underneath the humongous swamp buggy. "What the hell." Burt looked at Abner and then back again at the undercarriage. "There's no axle for the rear wheels." Abner just smiled, so Burt looked at the rig again, but but more closely.

"Don't need axles, Burt." He nodded towards the front, "I don't run but twenty miles an hour at top speed." He nodded again, "No need for front axle either." Seeing Burt's questioning frown, Abner explained. "All four tires are independant hydrolic pods, but I have control of them. I can lock 'em all together to operate like any other swamp buggy, or unlock all four or just the wheels I want to steer with." He pointed at the aluminum box that Burt had noticed hanging down below the center of the rear wheels. "That's the freezer, Burt. It's a half inch composit of high-tensile aluminum and aircraft-grade magnesium. And even though it's never happened, I'm sure it can take one helluva whallop without it suffering too much damage."

Burt turned to Abner, "Musta cost you a small fortune to put this rig together."

"Wasn't pocket change, Burt, but it didn't really cost me that much. I have a very good friend in Naples that's a retired mechanical engineer. After he designed it we started going to military lot sales, and got all of the main parts for pennies on the dollar. I worked with him for almost a year until it was ready for trial runs."

"Didja have a lot of problems to iron out?"

"No, not really. Mostly just a little tweeking here and there. He was part of the team that designed and built that first plane to carry paying passengers into space for a trip around earth."

Burt looked at the undercarriage again. "Ab, you've got a high-end, one-of-a-kind swamp rig here that oughta be able to take you anywhere in these Everglades you wanna go."

"Yeah, I agree. I knew I'd need a rig that would let me stay out there for long spells at a time to understand the habits of those snakes."

"Think you'll ever see the day when there aren't any pythons in the Everglades?"

"Weeeeell," Ab dragged the word out, "getting rid of them completely might be asking too much, but we can certainly get 'em under control, and then see to it that they never get the upper hand again," his eyebrows went up as he shook his head, "like they now have."

Burt mumbled, "I hope." He looked around, and then up at the huge I-beam running from one end to the other. He saw it was supported at each end and in the middle by large aluminum columns. Looking at Abner again, Burt said, "Good engineering."

Abner had already noticed Burt's eyes following the I-beam and said, "M'dad had that put in when the quonset hut was built. There's a moving winch in each of those steel boxes at both ends." He pointed to one then the other. "Either will lift the front or rear of the Swamp Castle, but we put an aluminum I-beam stiff-leg near the winch just t'be safe." He grinned, "Either end of that sucker's

Rick Magers

too heavy for a regular jack."

"Did you put those tires on it?" Burt just nodded at the Swamp Castle.

"Nah, I ordered all six from an outfit in Ohio. Two company fellas brought 'em on an open semi flat-bed loaded with special tools and jacks. They were already mounted on the rims, so all they had t'do was put 'em on."

"Must have been here a few days, eh?"

"I took her out that same day for a test run. That flat-bed had a big hydrolic snorkel-arm that snatched 'em off the bed and placed 'em right where they belonged."

While Abner checked something on the other side of one of those humongous tires, Engelburt stood nearby revolving his head to look at the inside of the half-barrel shaped building. When Abner came out, Burt pointed to a walled off area, "That your living quarters?"

"Yep, c'mon, I gotta get a few things before we head out into the Glades. You can look it over good while I'm putting my sack together."

"Damn," Burt said as his head swiveled inside the small apartment, "this's nice. Air condioner, full kitchen, compact little living room," he nodded toward a closed door, "and that must be a bedroom."

"Yeah, and my bathroom is in there, because I bring very few people out here. Those I do bring can either shit in the outhouse or head back to town." He grinned wide at Burt.

"Well," Burt commented as he continued on through the apartment, "if you like being a hermit then this is the perfect place."

"I'm not a recluse, but I don't see much value in being surrounded by a bunch of people that don't know which one's the hole-in-the-ground."

"Know whacha mean, Ab, because I'm surrounded by people who don't and never will. I live in an apartment house just a few blocks from the building where we put out the magazine."

"I ain't really anti-social," Abner said softly, "I just ain't comfortable around a buncha babbling people that never say anything worthwhile."

"You're sure as hell set up great." He pointed at the air-conditioner mounted next to the door they had just walked through. "You must have put that air conditioner through the inside wall to keep thieves from knocking it out and ransacking the place?"

"Yep. Dad had three huge spinners mounted on top to suck out the stale air in the Quanset, so the A C works great, with those spinners up there pulling fresh air in through the vents dad also put in. An old pal named Leon, a friend of my dad's, lives out back," he nodded, "in a trailer we set up for him and Susie."

Rick Magers

"Hard to imagine a woman living out here."

"Depends on what kinda woman it is."

"Yeah, I reckon it does. Leon and Susie out there right now?"

"Nah, I called and told him we'd be here today for a while. He's shopping in Naples. Leon doesn't drink or smoke, but when he gets low on apples he gets a bit cranky." Abner grinned, "Not really, just jokin, but he sure loves apples. I go up to North Georgia every year to visit an old pal on his birthday, and I always time it for when the apples are in."

"Sounds like you've got a good couple t'look after the place when you're not here."

"Yeah," Ab nodded, "I know how lucky I am to have a few good reliable friends like Leon." He paused before adding, "And Susie."

"You got anything else to check out before we head on out into the Glades?"

"Nope," Abner answered, "I brought all the groceries out here yesterday evenin, and after puttin 'em away, I topped off the fuel tank. Climb in and I'll take one last look around n' we'll be on our way."

Burt went to the ladder button that Ab had pointed out. He pressed it and stood back and watched as the door open down and the ladder begin unfolding.

Abner had told him that he got the entire unit from an older executive jet that another plane had hit while taxiing to the main runway. The impact tore off the tail assembly and a few feet forward. The plane was too old to invest in a new tail section, so they sold it to a parts outfit in Tampa.

They told Abner on the phone that the door and the folding ladder were undamaged, and the hydrolic system still worked. He paid the guy $1500 and drove back from Tampa with it in the back of his pickup.

Burt walked up the steps and looked around until Abner climbed up and hit the CLOSE button. "Man," Burt said, "there is more room in here than I would ever have thought possible."

Abner paused and looked around. "Yeah, by golly" he mumbled, "there is, ain't there? Guess I just take it for granted. Took almost a year t'get it all Engineered so it would do what I wanted it to, and then six months for us to build it." Once the door/stairs closed, he waited until the green light turned red and then pulled the lever that caused a steel rod to run through two eyes on the door so it couldn't fall open.

"C'mon," he motioned, "let's go up to the bridge and get on outa here."

Burt followed him up a straight up and down ladder bolted to the front left wall. Abner shoved the hatch up and went on up the ladder.

Burt climbed into the wheelhouse and just stood there rubbernecking. "This rig," he finally said, "is incredible. Looks like a wheelhouse I'd expect to see in an eighteen hundreds riverboat on the Mississippi."

"Hmmmm," Ab said softly as he stopped and looked around, "never thought about it like that, but I bet it does. Never saw one m'self, but it probably does."

"Trust me, it does," Burt replied, "I've been on one, but I've got a question, where's the steering wheel?"

"Right here in my hand." He held up a small remote that resembled a TV clicker. "Well," Abner said with a wide grin, "let's get this ship movin'." He climbed into the plush captain's chair, and after firing up the huge diesel engine he checked his instruments. Abner then pressed a button on the remote he held and the giant swamp buggy moved slowly toward the opening door.

Once it was outside he stepped to a rear porthole and watched to be certain the door rolled all the way down. Back in the captain's chair Abner manuvered the gigantic swamp buggy through a cleared road and entered the Everglades.

Half an hour later he climbed out of the chair and opened the propane powered refrigerator. With a round container in his hand he asked Burt, "You want an edible enema?"

Burt squinted and leaned forward. "Prunes. Nah, I'll pass. You get plugged up?"

Rick Magers

"Nope, always liked the taste of them plums and prunes. A purdy good side effect though is they keep the plumbing working."

"Speaking of that," Burt said, "is there a toilet on this Swamp Castle?"

"Sorta." He turned toward Burt and chuckled, then climbed out of the chair again. "C'mere n' I'll show ya."

Burt stepped back so Abner could walk to a door in one corner of the rear wall. Burt watched as he opened it and stepped into a small closet-like room.

Abner lifted the seat on a normal looking toilet but with no water reservoir. He sat down and pointed at a stainless steel trash can and pressed a lever with his foot. The lid opened, "No paper or anything else goes in the toilet—piss n' shit only. All paper goes in the can, and when the Walmart plastic bag is full we tie a knot in it and store it in that box." He reached over and tapped a swinging door in the box beneath the small sink. "There's a padlocked door at the bottom that we can open when we get in. Then they're all be put into a small incinerator that Leon and I built." He nodded at the sink, "Ration the amount of water you use because the tank's only seven gallons, and it's for coffee, cooking, and everything."

"That generator," Burt asked, "supplies current for the freezers under the main floor, huh?"

"That's its main job, but it also keeps two huge NASA batteries charged. The radar, GPS, weather forecast, auto-pilot, and area-plotter are all twelve volt." Abner leaned forward, and after checking his log book, made some adjustments to his destination on the area-plotter.

When Abner leaned back into his chair, Burt asked, "That area plotter looks just like a regular roadmap, with individual trees and hammocks showing up in three dimention. Is it accurate?"

"To within a yard. I downloaded it from a NASA satelite, and then modified it to use here in the swamp." He turned toward Burt and grinned, "Took me the entire six months that we were building the Swamp Castle, but those nights after work have paid off tenfold already." He used a wooden pointer and tapped an area on the north side of the huge hammock he had told Burt was where they were going to begin. "Instead of dead-reckoning around looking for number thirty-one, which is where we're headed, the autopilot gets its info from the GPS and takes us straight to it."

"Pretty cool," Burt commented as he watched the area-plotter. He straightened up and looked at the radar screen as the sweeping arm rotated. What's the main use for this?" He lifted a hand and pointed.

"If I gotta call Leon and have him come out in the airboat n' bring me som'n or bring the big Igloo coolers to take in some frozen snake meat to give me room to stay out a few extra days. I give him a course to steer. He puts up both outriggers with a radar cone on each so I can direct him straight to me. Saves me a lotta dough by

Rick Magers

being able to stay out here an extra few days."

"Looks to me," Burt said, "as though you have put together a pretty good operation."

"Ahm shore nuff a'tryin to git thar, ole son," Abner drawled out deep and artificially, "slower'n a turtle but sure as a fox."

"Keepin them hunters off your trail too, I reckon." Ab just grinned.

~ O ~

Several months later, the owner of the salvage vessel visited Limon, and was picked up by the motor-launch. After three days on the site of the galleon they were working, he had the launch pilot take him back to Limon. He asked the pilot, "Do you know where Eduarto's wife and daughters' house is?"

"Yessir, I take them groceries and clothing that the crew chips in and buys. I also buy Angelina a toy every time I take a box of supplies to her mother."

The middleaged man looked hard at the young pilot, and then smiled slightly while shaking his head up and down, "That's very thoughtful of you."

"She's a really sweet little girl, sir, and she misses her daddy very, very much."

The man shook his head slightly and said quietly, "I'm sure she does."

The taxi driver had taken the pilot to Mrs. Galindo's tiny house several times, so all the pilot said was, "Jorge, we'd like to visit Missus Galindo and Angelina."

When they arrived, the man asked the taxi driver in Spanish if he could return in one hour. The taxi driver nodded, and waited until the door opened. He then pulled away.

The pilot and the boat owner were greeted warmly by an older lady who said Angelina was taking a short nap. "I am her aunt, can I make you gentlemen some coffee," she said in Spanish.

"That would be very nice of you," the man replied in her language. While she busied herself inside the small kitchen he glanced around the little living room and was pleased to see how clean and neat she kept their home.

Over coffee, he explained that the papers she had signed during his previous visit were approved. "You and Angelina and your aunt Ramona are now able to enter the United States of America as legal immigrants. My wife and I will sponsor all of you and see to it that you have everything necessary to begin a new life in our country."

Before he could continue, Christina began crying softly, and then looked up into his smiling face to say in broken English, "Thanks you, Misser Grayson." After drying her eyes she thanked him again, and then added in Spanish, "Angelina and I will never forget Eduarto. We are so thankful that Eduarto's aunt Ramona is coming with us, because she has always been like a mother to me." Christina wiped her eyes and then added, "We will have family with us. I will work hard to make a new life for us all in America."

The man smiled, "During the much-too-short time that Eduarto worked with us, he became more like a son than an employee. Our daughter and her husband own a hotel and fishing resort in Everglades City, a small town east of our home in Naples, Florida. My wife will drive you there, and if you like it, my daughter will give you a full time job. After you have been there long enough to know if you want to stay there, we will buy you a small house, so you and Ramona will have your own home to raise Angelina in."

Christina remained speechless as tears flowed from her eyes and on down across her blouse.

~ O ~

About the time that Chuck's senses sent him a loud red flashing cerebral *DANGER* message, which indicated he should shut down the huge engine that was causing the big airplane propeller to spin so fast that the boat was almost airborn—it happened.

Two months earlier a bolt of lightning had struck a huge cypress tree that stood a few feet from the others along the edge of a large hammock.

Rick Magers

Every airboat captain, including Chuck, knew where it was. The tree had busted off about three feet above the water and fell into the hammock among all the other cypress trees.

Even half straight, Chuck would have normally idled down long before he got near that cypress stump sticking up higher than his gunwale.

He wasn't even close to half-straight. He was about as stoned as a person could be and still stay on their feet—or ass, as was the case with Chuck. His left foot was on the aluminum brace that his seat was welded to, and his right was on the throttle—that was bottomed out.

The airboat was doing about sixty when it hit that cypress stump a few inches right of dead center. Chuck never wore his seat belt, so he was launched right over the four passengers.

Arleen, Joel, and Alan weren't lucky enough to be launched. The metal screen cowling and frame that held the huge airplane engine was not designed to absorb an impact causing the boat to go from 60 MPH to almost zero in one second. The entire frame busted loose and sent the Engine forward with the three-blade-propellar still spinning.

It landed right on top of Joel, Alan, and Arleen. In only seconds they were hacked to death like tourists at a Caribbean machete massacre.

Belinda was thrown from the boat into shallow water. When her stoned-out brain began functioning a little, she stood to find herself in water only a foot deep.

What little moon that would come out would not be seen for a while. In tar-black darkness she moved slowly away from the wreckage. Her feet were in Key West sandals and slid easily along the firm bottom. Her head bumped against a large tree hanging out over the water. She abruptly stopped and rubbed the spot on her head. Her drug-altered sub-conscience sent her brain a signal: *this is a dry hammock.*

Holding onto a limb of the tree, Belinda stepped from the shallow water onto a dry mound. She had only recently grown beyond the tom-boy stage of her life, and could still climb a tree faster than most boys. Bending back she tried to see how big the tree was, but the slight sliver of moon still hid below the horizon, keeping her in darkness.

*I wonder*, Belinda thought, *if there are any of those huge python snakes that I recently read about around here?* a brief pause, *hell yes they're around here. It said in the newspaper that there might be half a million of 'em in the Everglades.*

That thought helped straighten out the kinks in her drug addled brain.

Belinda began carefully climbing the tree in the darkness. What seemed to her to be an hour later, she was at and end of the thick limbs. *Guess I'm up near the top*, she thought and settled back into as comfy a spot as possible.

She was still too frightened to be sleepy, so she just wriggled back and began looking for running lights on an airboat. After an hour of straining to see lights on any kind of boat or swamp buggy, she chuckled softly to herself, thinking, *what would I do if I saw one, Yell? Sure, that's it, yell my head off. Shit! Most of 'em are as loud as any damn freight train I ever heard.*

While she had been climbing up the tree, Belinda thought she heard a soft cry. She stopped to listen, but heard nothing. Now, a half hour later or even less, though it seemed like hours, she heard it again, but slightly louder. When she twisted around toward where she thought the cry came from she spotted the sliver of moon. *A little light,* she thought and squinted in an effort to see through the muddy air around her.

"Oooooh, help, oooooooo."

"Chuck." No answer.

"Oooooooooooh, help."

"Chuck Daggolonie."

"Yeah," came a very soft reply.

Before Belinda's feet touched the ground she heard a scream like no scream she had ever heard in the movies or on TV.

A moment after stepping down from the tree onto the carpet of leaves she heard a noise directly behind her. Thinking it was one of her friends that had survived the crash she turned. The huge reticulated python that began heading toward her the very moment she started talking to Chuck, flipped a coil around her, and then began his suffocating embrace. She screamed only once before the second and then third coil was around her tiny, four-foot eleven-inch, ninety-pound-body.

~ O ~

**D**elvin watched the fathometer as it began showing 70 feet depth.

He leaned out both sides and looked in every direction. *No boats, good.* He checked his watch and then a glance at the western horizon. *It's gonna be dark in about an hour,* he thought.

He leaned down and shook his brother's shoulder. "Get up Greg, it's time we get these traps in the water."

Greg swung his feet out of the bunk and slowly stood. His injured hand was still swollen, so it took a while to coax a camel out of his pack. Once it was in his mouth, he put the pack back in his shirt pocket and dug into his greasy Levi's for the Zippo. With the lit camel between his lips, he stepped out of the wheelhouse and watched as Delvin began getting the rope and buoy ready for the first trap.

"C'mere Greg and help me get this trap up on the gunnel."

Once it was sitting on the gunwale, he had his brother hold the trap while he made certain the buoy and line were untangled and

Rick Magers

ready to be set. *Glad I baited these as I loaded 'em earlier today,* Delvin thought.

"Hold this trap, Greg, and don't let it fall over. I'll tell you when to set it and get another one ready."

He went to the bow and looked 360 degrees. *Not a boat in sight. They're all in at the dock by now.*

Returning to where his brother stood holding onto the trap, Delvin stepped up behind him. The heavy leather-bound lead slapjack swished briefly through the air and knocked Greg beyond senseless. His unconscious body folded and fell to the deck.

Delvin pulled the trap rope that was attached to the trap until he had 15 feet in his hands. He swiftly put two half hitches on his brother's leg and pulled them up to his crotch. After snugging them into a tight clove hitch, he lifted the body and tossed it into the water as he nudged the trap off the gunwale. Delvin played the rope out as the boat drifted.

Once he was back in the wheelhouse Delvin looked at the buoy to be sure, it was behind the boat. He put the engine in gear and entered a course to set the balance of the traps. After engaging the autopilot, he began carefully trailing the next trap's line. Once the 120-foot long line attached to the buoy came taught he shoved the trap off the gunwale into the water and readied another trap.

When all of the 150 traps were in the water, he turned northeast, and after punching Everglades City on the GPS he engaged the autopilot again. Tears came into his eyes when his mind flashed a picture of his brother tangled in trap line a few yards above a stone crab trap sitting on the bottom in seventy feet deep water. *See all the shit and grief you caused, daddy, by stickin your pecker in Lulu? Shame they didn't shove the needle in you for killin' that young boy you thought cheated you out of a little cocaine.* He plucked a Puff Plus from the box beside the wheel and wiped his eyes. *I bet someone in there cancels your contract before you're paroled. I sure's shit hope so.*

~ O ~

The first explosion brought Ronnie out of the fogbank he had been in. He scrambled back until he turned and got his feet under him. Before he got far, Burt grabbed him yelling, "Hey, it's okay kid, we're gonna help you get home."

Both, fright and fight, left Ronnie when he looked up into Burt's eyes. He fainted and went limp as a fresh cadaver. Burt eased him to the ground as Ab continued putting copper slugs from his python into the huge writhing and twisting python a short distant away on the ground.

Ronnie was finally brought around, and was standing after cool water was rubbed on his head and face. After a while, he was able to tell them the entire story.

"Okay kid," Abner said soothingly, "I know where your friend met the python. We'll go to my swamp buggy, and while you rest and eat a bite, I'll go check out that area and see if I can find anything. I'll tow your airboat in, and you can come and get it any time you want."

So softly that neither man heard every word, Ronnie said, "You won't find any of Ziggy, because the snake ate him."

Burt and Abner looked at each other. Burt still had his arm around the boy. "C'mon kid, let's getcha som'n to eat and you can lie down for a while."

Once Ronnie had drank plenty of water and ate some of the assorted filled crackers that Abner always kept on the Swamp Castle, he crashed in Burt's bunk.

Abner motioned with his head for Burt to follow him out. When they were on the ground, he said, "Burt, There's no reason to check out the area the kid's takin about because I know it well. There's more big pythons there than anywhere I've seen." He looked into Burt's eyes, "It's a heart breaker, but there's nothing we can do but get this boy in so a doctor can check him out. I'm gonna go take some pics, because I casually walked off its length, and I think it might be the biggest one yet. Maybe when it's displayed in the newspapers the people in government that have the clout will start pulling some strings."

"What can they do?"

"Start teaching the guys that're gonna hunt 'em, and then we'll
Rick Magers

hafta convince 'em to pay 'em good. Our guys out here are the only hope there is to get these damn things under control." He looked at Burt and twisted his pursed lips while shaking his head, "Before it is too damn late."

Abner thought about it and realized the area where Ziggy had been attacked was only a fifteen-minute walk. He decided to go check it out after all.

Before he got to the area, Abner pulled his Python out of the holster and checked the cylinder to be certain it was full. He quickly scoured the area but found only Ziggy's jungle hat, but he decided not to mention it to Ronnie. He folded the hat, shoved it behind his belt, and covered it with his tee shirt. He would give it to the Park Ranger Station when they got in.

~ O ~

"Leon and Sissie are back. That's their pickup." With his head he nodded, and Burt looked in that direction and saw a very old Ford pickup truck. "He looks like a guy that doesn't trade in his vehicle very often."

"I took him to the Ford dealer," Ab said, "to pick up his new truck when it arrived. His old Model A Ford finally gave out. That two-thousand Ford over there," he nodded at the black pickup, "it ain't got but a bit over forty-thousand miles on it."
Rick Magers

"Damn, he stays pretty close to home, doesn't he."

"Yep, ole Leon ain't never been one to go traveling since he retired."

"What did he retire from?"

"Army, thirty years, and most of 'em as a Ranger."

As Burt was about to ask Abner something else, he noticed the trailer door opening. A short, thin old man stepped out followed by a huge black Rottweiler. He watched as Ab shook hands with the man. Burt watched the door thinking Susie would come out any minute. When he noticed Ab squating down patting the dog on his humongous head and saying Susie this and Susie that, Burt just smiled.

Ab introduced Burt to Leon who surprised him with a steel-vice type of handshake. "I was smiling a minute ago when I realized Susie was your dog instead of the wife I thought she was."

The skinny old man just laughed. "I'm sorta like them there old maid catholic ladies what wear them funny hats. "Ain't never had nuuuuuun," he grinned dragging the word out slowly, "ain't gonna git nuuuuuun, cause I damn sure don't want nuuuuuun."

Burt said, looking around, "You and Susie sure have a nice place to live."

"We both love it here, but I think ole Susie would croak if we had to leave."

Ab patted the old man gently on the back and put his hand on a shoulder, and then hugged Leon. "You ain't ever gonna be leavin' here as long as I'm alive."

Burt could easily see, by the way the old man smiled, that their relationship was a pure one based on solid trust.

~ O ~

Jintan met Amad at the main airport terminal in Bogota, Colombia. He had called Amad to relay a message from don Boris Aldenado, the ruling drug tzar of South America.

Jintan always used a sheet of code whenever he called Amad from an unsecured telephone. It was compiled by Amad's sister, also an extremely devout muslim and life-long terrorist. He told Amad that it was imperative that he come to Bogota immediately. Jintan watched the Learjet land. As it taxied on toward the private, executive air terminal in Bogota, Jintan stepped onto the moving walkway heading there.

During the short drive to the Hotel Tequendama, where Jintan had secured a large suite on the top floor, he immediately began explaining why he had summoned Amad.

"I brought you here, Amad," Jintan said, while slowly shaking his head back and forth, "when Boris Aldenado called and asked me to stop by his office. He told me that the Beechcraft King Air, which you bought from him and was planning to use for this mission, crashed during a test run." Jintan paused when he saw the look on his friend's face. When the frown was replaced by scrunched down eyebrows and pinched lips, Jintan continued. "He has offered to let us use his own personal aircraft, and he will personally see to it that the insurance company pays you promptly, because his brother owns it." Jintan was very glad to see that his friend's facial expression had changed; wiping out the desperation and horror that was there a moment earlier.

"What kind of aircraft is it?" Amad asked.

Jintan pulled a notebook from his suit's inner pocket, "A Grumman Mallard seaplane."

"Hmmmmm, that is the type that Chalk Airlines used when I lived in Miami. They flew passengers to Bimini Island in the Bahamas. I flew over with them on a free weekend when I wasn't so busy, and as I remember, it was a twin Engine and carried about a dozen passengers plus their luggage." He looked at Jintan and shook his head, "Yes, it will easily carry all five of the men, our equipment and the two hundred kilos of cocaine that I bought from him so he isn't aware of our main purpose. It will be boxed the same as our devices, and will recover some of the money used for our mission."

"It might actually be a better plane," Jintan offered, "since it can land in the Everglades with no danger of damaging our equipment. And then it can immediately take off again."

"Yes," Amad said while slowly shaking his head, "it would be disasterous if our pilots landed in deeper water and then the fuselage filled, ruining everything we've worked toward this past several years."

"Allah," Jintan said softly, "has been looking after us well as we struggle to rid our country of those American infidels." Jintan's face seemed to glow as he smiled at Amad. "Iran will soon be a country of united muslims."

Both men were silent for a few moments, as Amad digested the new wrinkle in the current mission. Finally he turned toward Jintan and asked, "don Aldenaldo is having the Mallard checked out thoroughly?"

"Yes Amad, it is now in his private hanger at the airport in Barranquilla, and his personal crew is checking it out as we speak. He is very careful about seeing that all of his business contacts are treated fairly and recieve flawless service. If there was neglect in connection with your King Air crashing, then someone will wish they had payed a lot more attention to detail."

Amad met with don Aldenado the following day, early in the morning. By noon he stood next to his aircraft talking to Jintan. "I believe, brother," Amad said, turning toward Jintan, "it was quite fortuitous that your brother's wife was born in Bogota. Her act of connecting us with Mr. Aldenado will be praised by Allah, and she

Rick Magers

will forever be remembered by all true Muslims."

A short time later, Amad was high above the clouds in his Learjet, heading northest toward Miami. Jintan was in a Learjet that he had chartered in Bogota, which was heading towards Barranquilla, Colombia. He wanted to be where the Mallard was currently being prepared for a very critical historic mission the following night.

During the final meeting with Amad and Jintan, Jerome said, "We tested the GPS beacons and they worked perfect."

Amad shook his head, "That's very good, Jerome, you dropped them from your own plane?"

"Yes, I took my brother-in-law, Milo, along. He's the mechanic I told you about that will be running one of the airboats. We tossed them out just before dark with one of the other airboat drivers watching the area to be certain that nobody was nearby to see us drop them. I have both locations in my plane's GPS, so we can drop them exactly where they should be, on the night the plane will be coming."

"And you checked them out?"

"Yes, Amad, we flew around Naples to Goodland and on down to Everglades City until it was dark. We came back to the area and turned the beacon on, and flew straight to it. I hit the switch and both lit up fine, so I came around and lined them up and flew from the one to the other and it went perfect."

"Very good, Jerome. Everything appears to be set to go on time in Baranquilla, so I'll keep in touch with you." He turned to Jintan, who had not uddered a word during this brief meeting. Let us get back to the office and see if any important calls have come in."

Jintan stood and held his hand out toward Jerome, "You are doing a very thorough job, my brother. Allah will reward all your efforts." Jintan's icy wolf smile made Jerome shudder inside as he shook the dark Iranian's offered Jintan hand.

Jerome watched both men leave. Standing there, he thought, *A great military horror movie could be done about those two.* His thoughts almost made him smile, *Wolfmen meet all of Uncle Sam's two million kids.*

Actually, Jerome hadn't yet done what he told Amad he had. *I better get Milo,* he thought, *and toss 'em in the swamp tomorrow night t'be sure they work.* He unlocked the door and slid onto the leather seat of his 2019 Dodge Super-Ram delux-cab pickup truck. After starting the gigantic, fuel-guzzling diesel, he sat there staring through the windshield for a long two minutes. *God,* he thought, *help me through this one and I'll never get involved with anything like this again.*

Jerome looked at his watch, and then hit 2 on his speed-dial. When Milo answered, Jerome said, "Check out the plane and top off those tanks. We're gonna take those two beacons out tonight n' toss 'em into the swamp, so I know for sure they do what they are supposed t'do."

~ O ~

The article in the Naples newspaper didn't hurt Jake Brown's business at all. "It might have even helped me," Jake told Gerald Proctor when he stopped by City Hall to drop off some papers.

"It's probably like people risking their lives," Gerald said, "when they slow down on a busy highway just to rubberneck a bad car crash."

"Probably so," Jake answered. "Here's a copy of my brand new liability insurance. At my lawyers suggestion I went by the insurance company he uses, and got one million dollars of liability for just a little more money than I was paying for half that amount." Jake pulled another sheet from his briefcase and handed it to the Mayor. "This is the name of the security officer that I hired to be the tail man on my walking tour. He graduated from the Miami Police Academy, but resigned after a year, and he and his wife moved back to Naples, where he was born."

"Didn't like police work?"

"He said he liked it but neither of 'em liked Miami."

"I can understand that. I could never live in a big city after I've spent so many years here in paradise."

"He's licensed to carry a weapon, and is a Black Belt in Karate."

The Mayor read the sheet. "Morris Whittaker, hmmm, sounds familiar," Gerald mused, "maybe he's related to an old Naples pal of mine named Joe Whittaker. I'll ask him when we meet." He looked up at Jake, "Y'still makin plans to have two new walking tours?"

"Yeah, I've got two new people that are interested. A guy about my age that run his airboat all over the Glades until they made it illegal, and a gal that wants the job so bad that she's paid six times to go with us. She's thirty and in good shape, because she runs in marathons every winter."

"Sounds promising, Jake, hope it works out for you. Let me know if there's anything I can do to help."

"Willdo, Gerald. Gotta run, because I have a tour of thirty-seven at noon." He waved and headed toward his truck.

~ O ~

The telephone console in agent Samson Blackraven's office began flashing. "Yes, Pablo, what's up?"

I've got the latest intel from Jerome, Chief, and I'm certain you'll wanna hear it."

Pablo Garcia entered Samson's office a few minutes later. Laying the folder on his desk, he said, "Took a while, Chief, to convert it all from his coded email, but his idea of what is going on coincides with what we recorded earlier during his recent meeting with Mister Gold and Mister Silver.

After listening to the recording, and then reading the file brought in by Pablo, Samson Blackraven slowly closed the folder and looked up. "I doubt Jerome will ever get involved again in any smuggling if he can live through this." His lips squinched a bit and his eyebrows went up. "Pablo, if Jerome can stay alive, then I am going to advise the court that he receives clemency. His big plan to smuggle in a ton of high grade cocaine never came to fruition anyway. I think we'll have a model citizen."

"Well," Pablo said, "if he doesn't forget to put on the shirt we gave him so the Navy SEALs can see him through their night-scopes, then he'll have a better than average chance to survive."

~ O ~

**R**upert Sedgewick, the number one man of the United States National Park Service, called a meeting in June, 2020. Only his top executive in Florida was notified to attend.

At 5:00 AM his Cessna Mustang landed at Tallahassee Regional Airport. The governor's limosine met him at the airport with Governor Skip Halsey sitting in the back.

Rupert climbed in and shook hands. "How you been doing with

this wicked heat, Skip?

"Stayin the hell out of it, Rupe. I noticed y'all ain't havin many cool days up in DC either."

"Hot's an AWOL Nun at a hunting camp." He turned toward the governor, who he had gone through college with, and grinned.

"I can see that you haven't lost your touch for graffic description." The governor just smiled then asked, "This meeting about the pythons in the Glades?"

"Yep, and everything's gonna be okay if I can just stop that land development company out in Texas from interfering."

"What're they up to now?" Skip had pulled a bottle of 50 year old Speyside Single Malt Scotch Whisky out of the liquor cabinet and poured a healthy amount into a tall glass filled with ice cubes and handed it to his college friend.

"Those bastards," Rupert said, "have hired lobyists to attend all meetings about those pythons here in Florida, and also up in DC." He took a long slow sip of scotch, and then added, "They're trying to prevent you from allowing that friend of yours down in Everglades City to go anywhere he wants to in the Everglades to kill those snakes."

Skip lowered his glass and said, "They want those snakes to keep multiplying until all wildlife is gone." He lifted his glass to take a sip and his friend followed his lead. "And then," he continued, "their plan is to make a big national issue that pythons

Rick Magers

are a hazzard to the population of the southern states. My spy inside their outfit told me they then plan to offer a solution, which is to drain and then fill the entire Everglades. The snakes that aren't killed by the fill," they'll claim, "will be killed by professional hunters on their payroll following the trucks." Skip Halsey shook his head of natural surfer-blonde hair; the envy of every surfer that relied on peroxide to give them that 'beach-bum' look. "The thing that really frosts my balls is that they'll probably win."

"Yeah," Rupert Sedgewick agreed, "and I won't be surprised if I'm still in my office when they fill the entire Everglades and begin creating dozens of golf courses, gated communities, and residential communities with thousands of plush homes, plus self-contained shopping centers, medical centers and hospitals so the residents will not have to leave." He said it all in one long breath, and then sighed, shaking his head before sipping his scotch.

"I'm afraid you're right on the money, Rupe. Those damn huge land developers have created enough clout to get nearly any project they want done—done."

"Their first big project will probably be Disney World South. That way they'll be able to get the green light to make Tamiami Trail an eight lane highway."

"Oh shit," Skip groaned, "and all those old timers that're buried around Ochopee, Everglades City, and Chokoloskee will really be spinning in their graves."

Rick Magers

Rupert Sedgewick slowly drained his glass and then shook his head. "One of the percs of getting old is that when you're really fed up with all the bullshit and greed, the lights go out and you're on the way to your next duty station."

"Welllllllll," Skip drawled with a grin, "if you are right, I hope to hell mine is on a planet where the oceans are beer and beaches are salty pretzels."

"Mmmm," Rupert mused, and then he pursed his lips and raised his eyebrows, "until that day comes, let's do all that we possibly can to stop those greedy bastards from filling in the Glades, and screwing up our beautiful state." He paused with his glass halfway up, "The land developers have been trying to fill the Glades for a hundred years, so I reckon one day they'll succeed."

Skip agreed, and then turned toward Rupert, "Are you going on down to Key West to see your folks?"

"Yep, soon as we get with your guys so I know we're all on the same page about this python thing. Then I'm flying down to visit for a couple of days."

"How old's your daddy, now?"

"Hmmmmm, I'm sixty-nine on November second, so daddy's eighty-nine and mama's eighty-eight." He then puckered up his lips, "Time sure flies when you're havin fun, huh?"

"Yep! Know whacha mean, Rupe. Don't seem like it was that long ago when we were both boys working on his shrimper down

Rick Magers

around Fort Jefferson."

Rupert was silent for a brief moment, but then smiled wide, "You remember that trip with him to the shrimp grounds down off Campeche, Mexico?"

"Oh yeah, how could I forget? We each made three grand, and thought we'd never hafta work again."

The two old friends rambled on, over good scotch as the limo headed toward the Governor's Mansion.

~ O ~

Skilleen Moshhanii emigrated from India in the mid 90s. His brother, a lawyer up in the Big Apple, took him along when he and his wife went to Marco Island on their vacation. It was only a beach and a swamp, just a bit south of Naples back in the 40s, but is now home to many of the super-rich. Skilleen scouted around for a job while his brother and wife went shopping in Marco's exclusive high-end fashion district.

An extrovert that had never met a stranger, Skilleen's natural self-confidence impressed the owner of a tour-bus fleet, when Skilleen applied there for a job. His six buses carried tourists from Naples to Ft. Lauderdale, Miami, and Everglades City.

The man, Yurrik Vittavitch, also an immigrant thirty years previously, hired Skilleen Moshhanii to operate one of his tour busses. Yurrik chose the Everglades City, Chokoloskee tour. The owner was a man with the kind of contacts that got things that he wanted, done. He helped Skilleen locate a small apartment in Naples near his bus depot, and then enrolled him in a state sponsored tour; Driver's Education and Application Course. If Skilleen could complete the course, he was guaranteed his Florida commercial driver's license.

Four weeks after his older brother and wife returned home from shopping, they received a call from Skilleen. "I will be taking my first bus full of tourists to Everglades City tomorrow. I thank you both for encouraging me."

Ten years after that first bus load of tourists, Skilleen bought the company. Fourteen years later he knew most of the people that lived permanently in Everglades City and Chokoloskee. He was well liked due to his energetic approach to satisfying his customers, and the fact that he still drove the Everglades City tour himself.

Skilleen was a short man who didn't quite hit the five foot mark and never weighed a full one hundred pounds. What he lacked in height and weight though, he made up for with complete confidence in his ability to conquer whatever task he decided to tackle.

Skilleen had spent so much of his time being the best tour guide, and then later as the most efficient owner, he never found time to court a potential wife. All of his lady friends enjoyed his company, and also enjoyed dating a thoughtful gentleman. However, with marriage always being their main motive, they soon parted company in search of more promising husband material.

Skilleen stopped dating altogether when he turned 50 and began exploring the Everglades. He had wanted to see and experience the Everglades and surrounding areas ever since he began describing the one-of-a-kind area to his customers. While he drove them toward Everglades City, and then across the causeway to Chokoloskee, he told his tourists everything he had learned about the Everglades, but now he wanted to actually see it for himself.

He bought a one-man kayak and began exploring the Ten Thousand Islands archipelago on the days that he scheduled his back-up tour guide to sit in for him.

The first year, Skilleen paddled through the islands near Naples and Goodland. After a year of that, he felt confident enough that he scheduled himself a two-week kayak paddling vacation. Skilleen's starting point would be Port of the Islands, where he bought a home in 2016.

Port of the Islands was once called Remuda Ranch. It was a huge hotel and marina that sat half way between Naples and Everglades city. It's now a housing develop that occupies many acres on each side of Tamiami Trail.

Rick Magers

The homes are beautifully landscaped and the hotel and marina have been thoroughly upgraded to match the 21st century developments seen in nearby Marco and Naples.

Skilleen's destination was the homesite of a notorious man named Edgar Watson, who had supposedly murdered several people. For many years he had given his tour groups a brief synopsis of the events leading up to the citizens of Chokoloskee putting a pound of lead into Mister Watson one dreary October day in 1910. He had always wanted to make the kayak trip to Edgar Watson's homestead, a few miles east on Chatham Bend. He was about to do exactly that.

Even though many of his friends suggested that he form a group of his friends that also had kayaks, Skilleen refused to be part of a group. "I've been with groups," he said with a smile, "ever since I began driving a tour bus, and now I want to go alone and take my time."

Skilleen covered the roughly 12 miles to Chokoloskee in good time. He camped on one of the Ten Thousand Islands at the half-way point, according to his GPS.

The next day he pulled in and camped on a small island a very short distance south of the 100 year old, Smallwood Trading Post and Museum in Chokoloskee. Years earlier, before the trading post was built, Edgar Watson was gunned down right below it.

After a hardy breakfast of sea trout, which he caught within fifteen minutes of waking up, Skilleen broke camp and headed east toward Chatham Bend, a place which his chart indicated was about 15 miles east.

A 15 mph wind blowing out of the west had made paddling the kayak a breeze for Skilleen, who was small in stature but kept himself in tip-top shape. His gym occupied six hundred and eighty square feet on the first floor of his house, and he used it regularly.

He pulled in when he spotted a small sandy area on one of the islands he'd been paddling past. It was still a good distance to Chatham Bend, so he knew he'd never get there by dark. It was only five o'clock, but he wanted to set up camp early and then do some casting to see if he could catch a snook for dinner.

One hour later his tent was up and he was scrounging around his campsite for some dry firewood. A man of uncompromising self-confidence, Skilleen arranged the unlit firewood and skillet, plus the ingredients needed, so whenever he was ready to cook the snook, everything would be at his fingertips.

By dark Skilleen had caught three snook too large for his dinner and had released them. He kept the three pound snook he had caught moments after releasing a ten pounder. After fileting it, he rolled the filets in a corn meal mixture of his own making, to fry while his small pot of rice cooked.

Rick Magers

Skilleen awoke at dawn with his kidneys ringing the bell in his head. He slipped into his canvas deck shoes and unzipped the tent's door. After relieving himself, he briefly scanned the swampy area that began a few yards behind his tent. Skilleen was an avid photographer, and had been filling cards in his digital camera all along the way. He always grabbed it and slung it around his neck before exiting his tent. The 400X telephoto lense was on it as he gazed at the trees beyond the mangroves.

Skilleen's eyes were glued to the camera, while he was looking through his viewfinder. His thin brown fingers were busy adjusting the telephoto lense as he slid his shoes along the sand toward the mangroves.

He was so obsorbed with the wild orchids that he was observing, that the naturally camaflaged, twenty-three foot long, soccerball size, Indonesion python lying in the swamp ten feet away went unseen.

~ O ~

Ronnie Weingarten finally got up the courage to climb down from the tree. He was so stiff from sitting all night on the limbs, and then struggling to climb down. Ron was only able to walk a short distance, until he flopped down, and with his head hanging he began rubbing his legs.

Rick Magers

He heard a noise and raised his head. Ronnie was looking into the eyes of a monster like none he'd ever seen on television. His ruptured mind tried to warn him by screaming, *move, move, move, get up and run.* Ronnie sat there silently frozen to the shell mound and stared into the mesmerizing eyes of the prehistoric beast. His frail body leaned against his right arm, which was rigid and unflexing, while the fingers of his left hand dug into the hard-packed shells until they began bleeding.

The reticulated Burmese python that was eyeing him would later be measured and entered into the records. It was 37 feet long, and the body's circumference was 47 inches—another record.

Ronnie's eyes followed its eyes as the snake moved slowly back and forth, cautiously moving toward prey that it knew was still alive and potentially deadly. Ronnie could not move. He thought about moving his stretched out legs back closer to him, but they simply would not budge.

When the huge body moved over the mound and out of the water, Ronnie's frail body reacted and emptied his bladder and then his entire bowels.

~ O ~

After snapping several pictures of orchids, and birds that were awakening from a peaceful roost, Skilleen had returned his camera to the case, and was placing his telephoto lens in a pocket of the same waterproof camera case.

Just as he was turning to get his breakfast fire started, a violent explosion of salty water, mud, and sand, literally knocked Skilleen down. Too frightened to scream, the involuntary infusion of adrenaline had Skilleen scurrying like a panic-stricken land crab, backwards away from the thrashing beasts that were causing the maelstrom, only feet from where he lay.

Skilleen was up and on his feet, running toward his campsite, where he kept the $4,000, .25 caliber Colt Pony automatic pistol that he was finally licensed to carry.

He shook so badly that he couldn't keep the zipper going up, so Skilleen grabbed both sides and yanked the zipper open. Having difficulty breathing, Skilleen never-the-less grabbed the weapon and eased back out of the tent while trying to see in every direction. Cocking the gun, he took a deep breath, and very cautiously moved forward.

~ O ~

Abner and Burt only stayed one night on the Swamp Castle. Their first day was spent checking places where Abner knew the python eggs that he had been watching were close the hatching. He logged each nest's statistics into his small electronic logbook and shoved it back into his shirt pocket.

Rick Magers

Burt was busy entering everything he saw into the recorder that was on his hip in a cell phone size holster. The wireless mic was clipped to the outside of his shirt pocket. Speaking in a normal tone of voice, it picked up every word clear and distinct, but filtered out most background noise. Once back at his pad in Chokoloskee, all he had to do was plug the recorder into his laptop and flip a switch. The transfer from recorder to a data sheet would be accomplished in a few moments, and then later it could be printed.

It was getting dark by the time they finished eating and cleaned up the cooking area. Exhaustion led both tired men toward their bunks, but still being keyed up, Burt couldn't sleep. "Hey Ab," Burt said softly before flipping off his LED reading light, "y'ain't asleep yet are you?"

"Nope, I'm just lyin here thinkin about which nests I should check tomorrow before we head back toward the barn."

"What time are we heading in?"

"We'll be checking out a couple of the hammocks while heading towards home, so we won't break off until two o'clock. That should give me plenty of time to drop you off, and get to Naples n' take care of some business."

"Hey, Ab."

"Yeah."

"Do you think there's even a reasonable possibility that you guys who know these Everglades, can ever get these pythons under control?"

"These snakes," Abner said, "are gonna end up being a bigger problem than those hyacinth plants brought to Florida back in eighteen-eighty-four by Missus Fuller."

"Boy, that's saying a lot, Ab, because I did an article on the hyacinth, and the many millions of dollars it has cost Florida and a few other southern states so far to control 'em in all the canals."

"The big difference, Burt, is that those floating river lilies ain't killed anyone, but a drunk up near Pahokee when he thought it was a solid bunch of flowers, and decided to walk across them." He paused for a brief moment before continuing. "Control is now the key word, Burt, because just like those hyacinth, they're never gonna get rid of 'em, and that's how it'll be with these pythons, because government's always too damn slow to act." His hair wobbled across his eyes as he shook his head, "I knew how it was gonna go, so I've been taking videos of the Everglades n' everything out here for the last eight years."

"The government's chock full of men like my father, Ab. Their only true interest is in whatever makes their own goddamn bank account grow, so I'm afraid you're right."

"I'd rather be wrong, Burt, but I feel certain I'm not."

"Maybe," Burt said, "one day I can help you write a book about it and include some of your pictures. My boss, Yan Chen, has a lotta contacts in the publishing world, so I'm sure he could get it published for you."

Abner finished checking his nests early the following day, so by early in the afternoon the Swamp Castle was heading back toward his humongous Quonset. "Hey," Burt said while pointing, "ain't that the same airboat with a coupla kids in it that we saw out here yesterday?"

"Gotta be," Abner answered, "can't be two painted up like that with lightning bolts and two pirate flags flying."

"Think we oughta try to get 'em to slow down?"

The Swamp Castle was already on the pre-set GPS course toward home. Abner said, "Nah, we start playing traffic cop, we'll never have time to catch snakes."

Burt looked at him, "Yeah, they'd just wait'll we were outa sight, and then haul ass again."

Burt made a date with Maggie on her day off, so he was knocking on her door at seven AM as they had planned.

Her roommate opened it, "C'mon in Burt, Maggie's almost ready to go." She yelled to let her know that he had arrived.

"I'll be right there, Burt."

"I cut her hair this morning, so she had to shower."

Burt asked, "You a beautician?"

"I was a wannabe for years, but I'm finally a gonnabe, and can't wait to open my own salon," she grinned wide, "one of these days. I'm finally in the last month of my training at Collier

Coiffeurs, a private school for fifty of us wannabe hairdressers."

When Maggie came out, Burt whistled. "Wow, I like your hair."

"Me too," she hugged her roommate, "You sure did a terrific job Ginger, thanks a lot. Your first and last drink's on me next time you come in."

Burt was on his feet and still looking at Maggie's short hair. "Sure do," Burt answered to her asking if he really liked her short haircut. "It looks great and must be much more comfortable."

"It is, and I'm gonna keep it short. Just run a brush through it," a huge grin caused Burt's gut to quiver, "and I'm out the door n' on m'way to work.

~ O ~

**T**ommy Seegar was born in nearby Immokalee. His too-young mother had been a die-hard Yankee until she moved away from the kids she had been raised amongst. At seventeen, leaving Boston was the most traumatic event in her life.

Her mother, Ophelia Crandon, was part of Boston's upper-crust socialites and she expected her daughter, Chantal, to follow the rules and become a debutante, just as she had done.

Chantal and her mother never saw the same words regardless

how large the print on the page was. She had rebelled whenever her mother suggested that she do this, that, or the other.

Their arguments ceased the day that seventeen-year-old Chantal eloped with twenty-year-old Alan Seegar, who was the gardener's assistant. Alan lived in a small apartment above the boathouse, which was a short walk to the small house occupied by their gardener and wife.

The boathouse sat next to a canal that led to the Atlantic Ocean, a short distant away.

The family's chauffeur drove Chantal daily, to and from the private school that she had attended all of her life. Exiting the limousine, Chantal headed up the long sidewalk toward the front entrance, just as she had done every day. However, as soon as the big black limo was out of sight, Chantal returned to the sidewalk that ran parallel to the street, and began walking north.

Two blocks later, she turned when she heard the loud growl of Alan's unique mufflers. Stepping between two parked cars, she climbed into his 1982 Dodge pickup.


Ten years later, Alan was still driving the same old truck.

However, by then, Chantal was already so hooked on heavy drugs that at twenty-seven, she looked more like a woman twice that age. She was barely able to take care of nine year old, Tommy, and seldom left the forty-year-old trailer, where they lived across the Trail in Lee Cypress. The small settlement where they had their old trailer was only a couple of miles north of Everglades City on State Road 29.

During the trip south, Alan had married Chantal in Georgia. They were on the way down to Everglades City, where his uncle had offered him a job on his commercial fishing boat.

From the day that Alan met Chantal, he had always felt certain that once they were married, her wealthy family would give them enough money to set themselves up nicely.

When Chantal called from Everglades City to tell her mother that she was now married and had a little boy named Tommy, and was pregnant with her second child, her mother abruptly hung up the phone.

She told Alan what happened, and he began ranting and raving, then opened a second bottle of cheap rum. A short time later, Alan had downed half of a large glass of the warm booze. He growled, "Y'musta said som'n to make your mom mad, y'goddamn dumbass bitch. Ask me before y'do anything like that again."

Before the night was over, Alan had, with one punch blacked both of her eyes, busted her nose and split her lip.

Later, on down life's road, when Chantal's second baby was almost due, she asked Alan to take her to Naples so a doctor could check her out. He said no, "My mother had three kids and never once went to no goddamn doctor. In West Virginia, women just call a midwife to come help get the baby out.

Just a few days later, a neighbor heard Chantal crying loud, and called an ambulance. It rushed an unconscious Chantal to a Naples hospital. The dead fetus inside was removed, and Chantal floated between life and death for several days. The infection was finally brought under control, but any hopes that Chantal had for another child, ended in the hospital ER.

Eleven years later, Alan beat Chantal to death while he was drunk and was eventually sent to Raiford Prison in Northern Florida, to serve 99 years. The uncle his dad had been working for on a stone crab boat took in their son, Tommy.

The violent relationship that had been going on between his parents, which he witnessed daily, had left an indelible mark on Tommy's brain. He went through life dragging a lot of baggage, and soon began drinking moonshine. It was made up in North Florida and was brought down south by his cousin, Aldo, who, along with making shine, poached deer and rustled free-range pigs on private fenced-in land, and then made sausage out of the meat and sold it.

When Tommy was thirty-years-old, he bought the boat from the man who took him in when his dad was sent to prison. Aldo was the only man that Tommy took out on his trap boat. Whenever there was no other trap boat in sight, while he was pulling his 1200 stone crab traps, or the 1500 lobster traps that he had set out in the waters between Everglades City and Marathon in the Keys. They would also pull any other traps in an area where his showed a good yielding of crabs or crawfish, which is what locals call their lobsters.

Tommy was never caught pulling traps that were not his, but as always happens, rumors began spreading that he was a thief. When trappers saw his boat they would call other trappers out on the water that day and tell them where they were and which direction that Tommy was heading.

Abner Brown had heard the rumors, and he knew that Tommy had an old swamp buggy. Ab also knew that Tommy was talking about catching pythons. Abner was in the Chickee Bar sipping a beer one evening at Billy Potter's Seafood Junction, when he heard Tommy's loud voice. He looked north through the screen and saw him standing with two men and two women.

"Yeah buddy," Tommy said in his tinny, high-pitched cracker voice, "them snakes're gonna be history fore to goddamn long, cause I'm dockin m'trap boat n' goin out there in m'airboat to start wiping those suckers out."

Rick Magers

*That's just fukin great,* Abner thought, *now that thieving asshole's gonna be running around out there.* He turned his head and watched as Tommy used both of his hands to embellish his story. *He looks like a damn pelican that ain't shit in a week tryin to get off the water to fly. I better give Skip Halsey a call and see if he can prevent Tommy from getting a python license.*

Abner Brown kept every bit of his python business to himself and never took anyone but Leon with him, and then, only when he needed a second set of hands. Leon delivered all of the python meat to a huge Ft. Lauderdale warehouse that specialized in exotic meats. They stored the skins inside freezers at the Quonset hut, and later, once they were all full, a Miami dealer picked them up. He took all of his python heads directly to the Everglades National Park warehouse in North Naples, rather than the new warehouse in Everglades City where they had a walk-in freezer to store them.

Consequently, very few people, in either Everglades City or Chokoloskee, knew that he was one of the few people that were licensed, and allowed to go anywhere in the Everglades by airboat or swamp buggy to kill the pythons.

When Tommy no longer had an audience outside, he staggered back into the Chickee Bar, which was now full. People were standing behind every occupied barstool, sipping a drink until someone got up to leave. Abner had given his stool to an elderly woman who came into the bar to speak to a friend that was sitting and listening to a local country singer, who was set up in the corner with his guitar.

Tommy saw Abner and moved in, to stand next to him. "Hey there, Abner," he slurred, "when are y'gonna run outa yer daddy's buried drug money and go back to trappin crabs?"

Abner set down his bottle of beer on the bar before answering, "Probably about the same time you get smart enough to keep your stupid mouth shut."

Tommy tried to set his glass of whiskey on the bar, but when he let go, it fell over. "Shit, see whacha just made me do, y'goddamn fancy pants rich boy."

Tommy never saw the uppercut coming. Abner threw the short punch so fast that Tommy was laying on the floor out cold a few words after he opened his mouth.

A middle-aged woman sitting on the stool next to where Tommy lay looked over at Abner then down at Tommy and asked, "What happened?"

Abner replied, "I think he had a heart attack."

She turned toward the bartender, "Excuse me, sir, but this man just had a heart attack." She pointed down at Tommy. "I think you should call an ambulance."

Between the rum and the uppercut that Abner landed right smack dab on Tommy's chin, he was still out cold when the Everglades Ambulance loaded him for the trip to Naples.

Rick Magers

A month prior to Engelburt's arrival, Abner was driving the Swamp Castle to one of the larger hammocks where he had been checking several python nests. As he got nearer, he spotted Tommy's derelict old airboat. It had been run up into the brush a little farther than normal. *Tryin t'keep from being seen*, he thought. He glanced west and realized it was later than he thought. *Gonna be dark in less than an hour.*

Abner idled the engine and put the transmission into low gear, then allowed the rig to slowly creep forward a short distance beyond where Tommy's airboat was tied. He stopped where the green brush concealed his wooden walkway to the center of the hammock.

Abner quickly made his way through the mangroves to the airboat. It took only a moment to locate the ignition wire, and another moment to cut out a two-foot section of it. *I can always put it back for him later*, Abner thought, *if it works out that he ain't really stealing any of my snakes.* He glanced all around, and then headed back toward the walkway.

Abner backed the Swamp Castle out of the twisted mangroves and headed around to the eastern side of the hammock. He had called the Everglades National Park Ranger Station as soon as he was in the wheelhouse.

"That's right, Johnny, Tommy Seegar does not have a python

Rick Magers

permit." After a pause to listen, Abner answered, "Okay Johnny, lemme give you all those GPS numbers again just t'be sure, and I'll be lookin for y'all."

After repeating the GPS location again, Abner moved around the huge hammock about a mile, where all of the mangrove trees were much smaller. After tying off the swamp buggy to a stout mangrove, he shut down and waited for the National Park Rangers. Two weeks later, Abner spotted Tommy Seegar's airboat tied to the mangroves again. It was in almost the same spot at the same hammock.

*Just as I figured*, Abner thought, *it doesn't make a bit of difference to Tommy whether he has a license or not, he's gonna do just like he's done with the crabbers, let us do the work and he pockets the money.*

After Abner pulled the Swamp Castle up into the mangroves near his wooden walkway, he shut down and strapped on the gunbelt. Abner pulled the Python Colt out and checked the shells. Shoving the long-barreled pistol back in the holster, he pulled out his Ka-Bar and lightly touched the edge. After shoving it back in the sheath, he glanced at his watch. *Damn*, he thought, *later'n I thought it was. Better take m'night eyes too.*

After he clipped the fiberglass case holding his night-vision goggles to his gunbelt, Abner climbed down and went back to the walkway. Half an hour of brisk walking later, he could hear Tommy Seegar's loud voice. *Sounds like he is drunk and is talking to a*

Rick Magers

*ghost or the damn snakes.*

With less than an hour of good light left, Abner could see Tommy through the foliage, and watched as he cut a third head off of a python and tossed it with the other two. He then slit the skin from one end to the other, and it looked to Abner to be about 20 feet long.

Abner watched as Tommy peeled a few inches of the skin back, so he could shove the two hooks at the end of a rope attached to a tree, into the snakes' exposed body. Tommy then straddled the snake and began pulling back the skin as he used his small sharp pocketknife to slice into the muscles holding the skin to the carcass.

Abner eased back out of the dense foliage and headed back to his swamp buggy. By the time he drove the short distance back to Tommy's airboat it was almost dark. It took only a few minutes to untie the bowline on the airboat, and then attach his towline to the rear of it. Once he was in the wheelhouse it took but a minute to tow the airboat out far enough.

Abner pulled the airboat close and climbed on. Once the stern towline from Swamp Castle was attached to the bow of the old airboat, he went back to his wheelhouse and began towing the derelict airboat toward another hammock about two miles away.

After twisting the piece of ignition wire back together and wrapping tape around the splice, Abner tossed the bowline in the water and climbed back up to the wheelhouse. *Whoever finds it,* he thought, *will figure that Tommy got drunk again and just didn't tie his airboat good.*

Half an hour after stopping to drop off the airboat Abner was heading home to his Quonset hut. *I'm afraid,* he thought, *ole Tommy's gonna learn the hard way that there are more pythons out here than almost anyone is aware of.*

~ O ~

Skilleen was completely mesmerized as he stood less than twenty feet away watching a huge crocodile battling a giant python. It was a life or death struggle that went on for fifteen minutes. Each time the python attempted to get a loop around the crocodile, it would release its jaws to swing its head back and forth so furiously that the snake could not get the loop secure.

Finally, with a burst of muddied water, sand, and shells, the croc lifted the snake high enough to slightly release its jaws; just enough that the snake's body slipped farther back into the powerful jaws.

Skilleen shivered when he heard a crunch as the powerful jaws snapped shut. The croc began violently shaking its head from side to side, but this time the python was between the croc's teeth.

Skilleen's mouth dropped open when two sections of the snake dropped. The croc lifted up its head and easily swallowed the portion it had ripped out of the snake.

Rick Magers

He watched in awe as the croc grabbed the smaller section of the snake with the head attached. It was still writhing and thrashing as the jaws opened and closed repeatedly. Grabbing it in the center, the croc repeated its previous maneuver. After the two smaller parts, one with the head attached, fell, it lifted its head again high and swallowed the section that remained in its jaws.

Skilleen looked around to see if there was a tree that he could run to in case the croc decided that he looked like a tasty dessert. Seeing nothing, he quickly loaded all of his supplies and the tent too, while the crocodile was still enjoying its breakfast. Moments later, he was paddling furiously to put distance between him and the prehistoric beast he had been watching.

The adrenalin was still rushing through Skilleen's system when he spotted Chatham Bend, the site where the Park Rangers burned down Edgar Watson's home in 1960.

He paddled his kayak towards the dock. After tying it to a piling, he climbed out and stood on the dock. He stretched several times and then bent down to rub his legs until the circulation began flowing better and the tingling shakes ceased.

Seeing that he was alone, he pitched his tent on the shell mound between the trees that once shaded Mister Watson's rambling two-story home.

When Skilleen first began driving the tour bus, he once asked a local stone crab trapper who was born in Everglades City sometime around 1950, "Why did those Park Rangers burn down a piece of history like Mister Watson's home down on Chatham Bend?"

"Because," the old crab trapper said, "them simple minded turd smokin' bastards running the Everglades National Park wanted to flex their muscles and show us they were now in charge and could do any goddamn thing they wanted to."

Before Skilleen could say another word, the old crabber continued. "The same type assholes that gave the order to burn it, also promised to let all of the local commercial fishermen retain their rights to continue making their living in the same areas they and their forefathers had for almost two hundred years. When they closed off access to most of the areas we trapped, our lawyers at OFF," he paused, then remembered he was talking to an outsider, "Organized Florida Fishermen," he continued after explaining what OFF was, "took it to court." The old fisherman chuckled sarcastically with a snort out of his sun-riddled bulbous red nose, "Some goddamn judge finally settled it all." His eyes closed and he shook his head as he took a long deep breath. "He said som'n like, 'This situation runs along the same line as the treaties made with various tribes of Indians. It was good at the time it was written, but is no longer a valid argument, considering modern times.'

He coughed and spit bloody phlegm on the ground before lighting a fresh Camel from the half-inch butt he'd removed from his lips, then added, "Kinda makes a feller think them injuns were right on the money when a chief once said, 'white man speak with forked tongue.'

~ O ~

Skilleen got his camp set up and had his evening cooking fire all prepared. With the camera hanging around his neck, and the telephoto lens in a leather holster snapped to his belt, he began wandering around the property taking pictures.

An hour later, he was back at his tent looking up at a clear, cloudless sky, with the sun radiating his portion of the planet. "Mmmmmmm," he moaned, "a beautiful day for a swim to get the sweat and funk off of my body."

Ten minutes later, he was walking toward the dock in just his bathing suit. *A quick swim*, he thought, *and then I'll get my spinning rig and catch something for supper.*

Had Skilleen decided to catch his dinner before he went swimming, he might have changed his mind about a swim. His perfectly executed shallow dive caught the attention of one of the worst beasts in the local waters.

Skilleen did a short breaststroke out before turning back toward the dock, which was only ten yards away, but still far enough that he would never make it back to land.

The bull shark hit him right in the left hip, just as it would have a large snook or redfish, which to his sensors would have been about the size of the creature splashing along up on the surface of the bull sharks' food-hunting grounds.

Skilleens' only scream went unheard. A second, and then others joined the huge bull Shark. Moments after being hit by that first lone bull shark, Skilleen was torn  apart; each shark trying desperately to swallow the chunk of flesh and bone that it had ripped from the legless cadaver hovering below the surface of the muddy water. Once each bull had severed a chunk, it roared away at full speed to keep from becoming dinner for the dozen or more bulls that would show up within minutes of a kill, and attack anything in the water.

When the Park Rangers arrived the following day, they would find no clues that would explain the vanishing tour-guide. The film in his camera was developed, and even though the pictures of the crocodile and python were extraordinary, they offered no clue whatsoever to his disappearance.

~ O ~

Burt and Maggie had both been trying to get a couple of days away from their jobs to set up a real date, when the love gods smiled down on them.

Rick Magers

Burt would have three days off while Abner Brown was taking care of business. He was enjoying a sandwich at the Chickee Bar when Maggie said, "I'm getting two days off in a row, starting tomorrow." She whistled a sort of pheuewe, "First time in a while."

Without a second's hesitation, Burt blurted out, "Let's you n' me do som'n together, Maggie, cause I'm not goin out with Ab for three days."

"Sounds great," she answered while wiping the top of the bar, "whadaya think we oughta do?"

"Mmmmm," Burt mumbled, "well, there's something that I always wanted to go see over in Clewiston, but it might not appeal to you."

"What is it?"

"A Seminole museum up the road close to Clewiston named AH-TAH-THI-KI. I checked my GPS and it's seems only a little over a hundred and thirty miles."

Maggie smiled, "I've heard customers that have been there talking about it, and they all seemed to really enjoy the place. Yeah, I'd love to go see it."

Her smile brought out the poet in Engelbert. "Boy-oh-boy, I love that smile of yours, Maggie. It would make a dreary day sunny and a sunny day brighter."

She grinned mischievously, "Does that mean we're going to Clewiston, tomorrow?"

Rick Magers

"Yep! Whatever time you say, and we'll be on our way."

"There y'go," she smiled, "rhyming again."

"Must be me Irish side shining through, lass."

"You're Irish?"

His sly devilish grin made Maggie's stomach jiggle. Burt asked, "Are there Jews in Ireland?"

"Nope, they ate 'em all during the potato famine." She let out a huge laugh, and then continued laughing so hard she put both hands over her face.

Grinning at her laughter, it was his stomach this time that did a jiggle. Finally, he said, "I'm a born optimist, so I called the place and asked if they have a charger for Ford electric cars, and they do."

"After riding in yours I told my roommate and she said her uncle in Ft. Lauderdale has one just like it and loves it. He told her that charging stations are popping up all over in that area. He also said that the different companies that are now making electric models, all got together and made the chargers uniform to fit 'em all. Cool, huh?"

"Yeah, and now they're starting to pop up all around the greater Miami area, too."

"Maybe," Burt said, "that'll be a start at this being the United States of America, again."

Maggie paused a moment with the bar rag still in her hand. Finally she said, "Let's have a big breakfast at the Havana Café at seven tomorrow morning, and then we will head north up twenty-nine toward Clewiston."

"Sounds great, Maggie, I'll pick you up a little before seven." He drained his glass of tea and stood. "I gotta get my notes edited and in the manuscript now, so I'll stop by about four and have som'n to eat then give you a ride home. Your car's still in the shop, right?"

"Yeah, but I got lucky. The brakes were not as bad as he thought, so it's not gonna cost so much."

"It probably just needed to have a new set of shoes on all four, and a good cleaning while they were in there."

"That's what he said, and I can pick it up at five when I get off."

"Good, I'll drive you over there this afternoon after I'm through eating. It's on Chokoloskee, right?"

"Yeah, thanks a lot." She headed toward a couple of customers climbing up on stools at the end of the bar.

"See y'later," Burt said as he pushed the screen door open.

Burt finished his fried shrimp basket just as the evening bartender walked in to begin his shift. Ten minutes later, they were heading south toward Chokoloskee.

Rick Magers

Burt noticed that Maggie was quiet and seemed to be deep in thought, but he said nothing. As they crossed the bridge at the south edge of Everglades City, Maggie turned slightly toward Burt with a slight look of dread on her beautiful face.

"Burt, there is something I've gotta tell you, before we go off together tomorrow, and this new relationship of ours goes any farther."

A few things went rapidly through Engelburt's head. *She has a husband, a boyfriend somewhere, mebbe she's a lesbian.* He took a deep calming breath before speaking. "I like you a lot, Maggie, and you can tell me anything you want and we'll stay good friends."

She turned toward him and smiled, "You're really a good guy, Burt, and I like you a lot too. This might sound a bit bizarre or old fashioned, but it's something that I've thought about since I was a young girl." She took a deep breath herself, and let it out slowly as she looked at him. "Burt, I've only dated three guys in my life. Two were just casual dates to a movie and a bite to eat later, and one that lasted three months. That one ended when I told him what I'm about to tell you." She took another deep breath when he looked over at her.

"Maggie, I meant it when I said that I really like you. I have never met anyone like you, and I'm glad you like me too. Just tell me what's on your mind, and maybe we can discuss it and work our way through it, okay?"

Rick Magers

"Okay, Burt, here goes." She took a very deep breath this time before saying, "I am a virgin, Burt, and I have decided to remain one until I meet a man who has the patience to get to know the real me. I know sex is a big deal for men, and some women too, but I've seen firsthand the results of letting sex or any other one thing determine what type of relationship a man and woman are going to have, before they have time together to even begin to understand each other." Maggie took another very deep breath, trying to calm herself, and then said, "I'm not gonna let that happen to me, Burt. And if you wanna cancel the trip to Clewiston tomorrow, I'll understand, and we can stay friends on opposite sides of the bar."

"Maggie, I had brief relationships with women while I was going to college, and they all had one thing in common. They were all shallow. There was no depth to any of them, and certainly no love of any kind. They were all just extremely shallow relationships between two people trying to bridge the gap of loneliness for a brief time." He turned toward her, "And it never really helped. I walked away as lonely as when we met."

Burt took a deep breath, "I overheard my father one night talking to his business partners in the study while mom was visiting her parents. I learned that he got my mother pregnant, and then had to marry her or lose the opportunity to become part of her father's huge banking dynasty." He turned to Maggie, "They've detested one another ever since, Maggie, so I think you've made a very wise decision. I want us to be friends as long as possible, and in order to accomplish that, I see no reason whatsoever why sex should hafta be a necessary part of that friendship." Burt turned a sincere smile her way and added, "Okey dokey?"

"Sure." Maggie leaned over toward him and kissed Burt's cheek. "See ya in the morning."

~ O ~

Jake Brown left the Carnestown Sub Station feeling as though another hurricane had rushed on through his life, and then left only flotsam and debris behind. Collier County Sheriffs' Detective, Jiminy-Pa Roanoke Huntington, a friend who he had known since they were schoolmates in Everglades City. Their wives were good friends that had also gone to school in Everglades City, but Jake's wife, Betty, had been one grade higher.

One evening when Jake and Jiminy were enjoying some cold watermelon in Jake's back yard, he said, "I always wondered, Jiminy, why they gave you a middle name like that. Pa sounds like a Chinese name, or a name in India, but Maybelle and Russell sure ain't either."

Jiminy laughed and choked on a chunk of melon. He finally caught his breath and answered, "Mama told me that Russell's daddy, Rufus, told her a story one day while they were sitting on the porch. 'When Russell was a little boy,' Rufus said 'he always answered, when I told him that he had to do something, with, "Well, jiminy, Pa." Rufus and Pam never had another kid, but he always said, if they would have had another boy, he was gonna name him Jiminy Pa.'

"So," Jiminy said as he grinned at Jake, "like that ole radio fella named Paul Harvey that m'daddy had always enjoyed listening to, always ended with, "and now you know the rest of the story."

Jake smiled, "Females are kinda funny about naming their kids, so Maybelle musta liked the sound of it."

"Jake," Jiminy smiled, "mama liked Rufus so much, that I've always been glad that daddy didn't answer ole grandpa Rufus with, aw shit Pa."

Both men had a good laugh, and went back to their watermelon and fresh squeezed, Key Lime limeade.


Part of Jake's gray mood was because of what Jiminy had said to him earlier. It kept replaying in his mind like an old fashion record stuck on one line of a song. *Betty and I both have been encouraging you to hire someone to watch the rear end of your walking tour.* "Shit!" He said aloud while puckering his lips and shaking his head, *why in the hell didn't I listen to them.* His mind kept replaying that one line repeatedly.

Jake was starving, so he whipped into Billy Potter's and parked. He had made the arrangements to have his friend, Jack Shealy, who owned a camping resort and pole boat tour just east of Ochopee, to send one of his tour guides to the substation to drive the tour bus to Naples, so Jake's tourists could get on their way once they gave their depositions. He told Jack, "I'm in no shape to take 'em to their cars at my tour office in Naples, Jack, plus I'll probably be right here at the substation a while." He felt very relieved when Jack said he would send someone immediately.

"Thanks a lot, buddy."

"Any time, amigo."

An hour later, Jake watched as his customers climbed aboard his tour bus. He handed Jack Shealy's guy two twenty dollar bills and thanked him for coming. Thirty minutes later, his deposition was completed and he was heading towards a cold iced tea and a bite to eat.

Jack ordered and sat quietly sipping the tea until Maggie asked him if he was feeling okay. "No, Maggie, but once I finish my shrimp basket I'll feel fine."

He was usually chatting and in a real good mood, so when he sat sullenly sipping his tea, Maggie wondered what had put him in such a dark, silent mood.

When he finished his food, Jake ordered a beer, which he seldom did. The bar was empty when she sat the bottle down and picked up his empty basket. "Som'n has gotcha down, Jake," she said quietly, "I hope nothing is seriously wrong."

Jake, like nearly everyone else who lived permanently in EC or Chokoloskee, liked Maggie. He sat the bottle down, "Bout as wrong as it could get, Mag."

Maggie felt a wave rush through her when she saw Jake's lips pucker up, and his eyes close as he shook his head slightly. He glanced around the bar, and then knowing that she had never, as far as he knew, been one to contribute to the gossip-chain or helped to spread rumors, he said, "Mag," and looked again to be certain there were no other locals to spread it around town, "my tour........he briefly told her what had happened.

"Oh my God, Jake," she said almost whispering, "what a rough break, just as your tour is really getting good reviews in the Naples and Marco newspapers."

Jake was never big on sympathy or tails-of-woe, but Maggie always seemed to be the exception. She sounded sincere whenever he had heard her commenting about someone she knew that was having a rough time.

Maggie was wiping the bartop near Jake when he put the bottle to his lips and drained the beer and asked for second.

Fifteen minutes later, he placed a twenty on the bar to cover the two beers and climbed off the stool. "Things're gonna be better, Mag," he had a new, I feel good, smile on his face when he turned back toward her, "now that I've learned this hard lesson." He picked up the food check and headed toward the cashier.

On a beautiful sunny Saturday, a week later, Jake was inside the Havana Café on Chokoloskee, finishing a late lunch when Morris Fent walked in. The way he wobbled it was obvious he had been drinking heavily. When he snapped his fingers at the young waitress, demanding a menu and a beer, it was quite obvious to everyone else inside.

When Morris noticed Jake Brown paying his check, he yelled, "Hey there, walking monkey, did any more of your goddamn Yankee customers git eaten by them there pythons lately?" He snorted while he laughed, and then added, "Only a stupid asshole like you would walk a big buncha tourists through the goddamn swamp."

Jake paid no attention to his drunken ravings, because the man was known to have a bad case of diarrhea of the mouth whenever he drank, which was whenever he was awake. He silently paid his food check and walked to the adjacent Post Office to get a money order.

A few minutes later, Jake tucked it in his shirt pocket and left the building. He was almost to the door of his new Dodge truck when he heard Morris' voice..."What the hell's the matter with y'all? That joint of yours sure ain't no goddamn Chucky Cheese fer kiddies, f'Christ's sake."

The stout young man who had escorted Morris out, pointed a finger straight at him. "And don't bring your vulgar mouth back in here, More Ass, or you'll spend the night in jail again. And just like last time, More Ass, you'll spend all of your extra money just to get back to square one."

Just as the Post Office door was closing behind Jake, Morris swung around and slammed his left hand down on his right arm inside the elbow and fired a lone, middle finger missile, into the air at the young guy walking back into the Havana Café.

When Morris heard footsteps, he almost fell while turning around just as Jake was heading past him to get in his truck. "Hey, fuckwad," he slurred as he wobbled to keep his balance, then he grabbed Jake's left arm, "where the f…

Jake's right fist hit him in the gut so hard that Morris shit his pants. With Jakes' now-free left hand, he grabbed a fistful of the man's greasy Levi Jacket. While holding Morris up, Jake hit his nose twice and then his right ear as he was going down.

Jake was only breathing a little heavier than usual as he leaned down. "I don't usually lean on a worthless piece of shit like you, Morris, but like about everyone else around here, I'm fed up with you and your tough guy line of bullshit."

Jake took a few long steps and opened his door, but before climbing up onto the running board, he spoke just loud enough for

Morris to hear, "Touch me again and I won't just lean on you a bit. You'll be in ICU for a long vacation."

As Jake was backing out, Morris lay in the parking lot thinking, *lean on me? Shitfire, I hope the bastard never decides to really punch me.*

~ O ~

Engelbert picked up Maggie right on time. After they sat down, and had been given their menu, Burt watched the owner working at the big grill behind the counter. When Maggie asked if wanted to look at the menu, Burt said he was going to get the same thing he had a few mornings earlier.

"What's that?"

"Huevos Rancheros."

"I love 'em," Maggie said, "and Carlos makes the best I've ever had, so make it two." She stood and pulled an envelope from her purse, "Almost forgot to mail this. Be right back, so please order me a Cuban coffee, too."

When Maggie sat back down, Burt asked, "Carlos is Cuban, isn't he?"

"Yeah, but he makes Mexican food as good as, or maybe even better, than any Mexican cook I've seen. He's just an all-around cook, because he can make an apple pie as good as any my granny

Rick Magers

ever made, and he also makes the best darn, creamy lobster bisque that you're ever gonna eat."

"Ab said he's been around here for a long time."

"Yeah, he was fishing for a living out of here back in the 80s. He'd take a crew out on his boat back then to fish for grouper or snapper, and if a blow came up, he didn't head back in to the dock, like some. He'd drop anchor and ride it out then go back to fishing until his ice boxes were full." She laughed, "I heard that his crew bitched a little about all the weight they gained while fishing with him, because he cooked such good food during storms."

"Oh boy," Burt said, "speaking about good food." He picked up his fork as the young waitress placed their breakfast in front of them.

~ O ~

The museum exceeded their expectations, and it kept them busy visiting the many displays until two o'clock in the afternoon.

They stopped at a newly opened Mexican restaurant on the outskirts of Clewiston. A sign caught Maggie's eye when they drove past it earlier.

GRAND OPENING

FREE FLAN FOR EVERY NEW CUSTOMER ALL MONTH.

An hour later, they were heading back south towards the paradise they now called home, Chokoloskee.

"I honestly believe," Maggie, said, "Those were the best tacos that I've ever had."

"I agree, and they were the real Mexican type that I really love, but seldom find. Spicy meat in double corn tortillas with a bowl of chopped cilantro, onion, and salt to put in 'em, and a bowl of the best salsa I ever tasted, to add to 'em."

"Must be their own salsa recipe," Maggie added, "I've never had any quite like it." Maggie giggled, "We musta ate a pint of it with those home-made chips they kept bringing until the taco plates came."

"I don't eat a lot of rice," Burt said, "but their rice had som'n different in it. I could eat that rice with any meal."

"Those refries were different too," Maggie added, "I think I tasted cumin and cilantro paste, and that cheese I tasted in the beans was sure not generic cheddar."

Burt turned toward her and grinned, "Like that big ugly sucker that made sci-fi movies before becoming the governor of Californicate often said in his Russian or his Swiss, or whatever accent that was, I be bock."

Maggie giggled like a schoolgirl before saying, "That was Arnold Schwarzenegger. He was a world famous bodybuilder who came here from Germany. I watched a couple of his older movies,

Rick Magers

and liked 'em."

They drove along chatting about movies, food, places they hoped to see some day, and a dozen other topics as they became more familiar with each other's many varied tastes and dreams.

Burt and Maggie took a different route back. Instead of taking 27 down to I-75, they went west from Clewiston until they came to SR-29, and then they turned left and headed back toward Everglades City. Burt turned off the air conditioner, and brought down the windows so they could enjoy the fresh air.

They were pointing out to each other some of the rare wide-open areas of the state. Passing beneath I-75, they went less than a mile, when just ahead of them a quarter mile; a semi had hit something and nearly lost control, but was able to get straightened out and stop his rig.

Burt said, "That guy just hit a log lying across the road, and almost wrecked." Before they got to the truck, they could see the driver, who had climbed down, jump back on his running board and climb back into the cab.

When Burt stopped his car, they could both see that it was not a log, but a huge python that was still alive, and trying to get on across the road and into the brush and trees.

"Wow, this road's about seventeen or eighteen feet wide and that snake's head is in the grass on the west side and the tail's still in the grass on the east side. It must be over twenty-five feet long."

Rick Magers

"That eighteen wheeler darn near busted that snake in two, but look how it's still trying to crawl off into the woods."

Burt eased ahead and motioned for the driver to roll down his window. When the guy did, Burt yelled, "I'll call 911 to send someone to kill the snake, so if you don't want to get bogged down with paperwork, just haul ass while there's nobody on the road, and I'll tell 'em there wasn't anyone here when we saw the snake."

"Thanks, pal, I'm already running an hour late." The trucker nodded and headed north.

When a Florida State Trooper arrived fifteen minutes later, the officer agreed with Burt that the python was dying, but he still called his headquarters. After several minutes on his phone, he turned toward Burt, "My boss said to put it out of its misery, and then call animal care to come and measure it. They'll probably load it, so they can run tests and get some information." He pointed, "That tail's already worked its way up outa the grass, so you can probably get that car of yours around it." He paused a moment and looked hard at Burt's car. "That one of those new electric Fords that I've been hearing about?"

"Yep! Sure is and I love it."

"How far can you go between charges?"

"Two hundred miles, and they recharge while you're having lunch, plus the top is a solar panel that helps keep the batteries charged."

Rick Magers

"Got any pep?"

"I've only had it up to seventy, but it seemed to have plenty left if I needed it."

"Okay, thanks a lot, I'm gonna check into one, now that gas has once skyrocketed. And thanks for calling us about the snake, too." The officer looked hard at Burt's car, "What's that lump on the top?"

"That," Burt said, "is gonna put millions of lawyers out of business if it catches on, and becomes standard equipment on all vehicles. It's a three hundred and sixty degree camcorder that captures everything that happens to the vehicle it's on, and shows the GPS location, time and date. I ain't sure how it works, because there's no tape or recording wire, but all you do is hit rewind at night when you're finished for the day, and it's ready to begin again, and goes on when you turn the ignition key." Burt held up the car keys and added, "Before going into court, all you do is insert this flash drive and press SAVE, and the judge can view everything when he plugs it into his computer."

The young police officer removed his hat and rubbed his head, "This new world of electronics is really som'n. I believe I'll rethink my decision to work on a law degree online and on m'days off." He grinned, "Might be better off getting another degree in electronics."

"Good luck, we will be on our way, then." Burt waved and climbed in beside Maggie, who had run both of the windows up.

Rick Magers

They talked about the snake all the way home. Burt told her that it looked to him like Abner is correct about the urgency to get a plan underway to prevent pythons from eating all of the animals and birds. "If that happens it'll throw everything in the Everglades off balance, and it might be the beginning of the end for the Glades."

~ O ~

Tommy Seegar finished skinning his third python, and celebrated by downing a mouthful of Jack Daniels. After placing the quart bottle back on his jacket and leaning it against the gumbo-limbo tree, he rolled up the skin and tied it. After shoving all three skins in a gunnysack, he put the jacket on and then took another long pull on ole Jack's No. 7.

The gunnysack was so heavy he had to drag it along Abner's wooden walkway towards his airboat. When he reached the end of the walk, he pulled a small flashlight out of his jacket pocket and shined it through the foliage. *What in the hell*, he thought, then left the sack of skins and stepped off the walk and waded the twenty feet through the mangroves to where his airboat should have been.

Tommy stepped out of the mangrove roots, and then waded on out until water was half way up to his knees. He shined the light along the edge of the mangroves, first one way and then the other. *I*

*tied the damn boat to the mangroves roots right here — I think.* He paused a moment while he strained his brain, and then his eyes to see left and right. *I'm purdy sure I tied the damn thing right here.* When he shined the light along the rapidly darkening shoreline mangroves one more time, he noticed that the light was beginning to get weak. After sending the dim beam again in the other direction, his thoughts were more about the darkness he was now in than his missing airboat. *Goddamn light's givin out n' this sure's hell ain't no place t'be without any light.* Tommy waded back to the walkway and climbed up on it. Before picking up the sack, he looked up at the sky. *If m'figurin is right, there ain't gonna be no damn moon atol tonight. Shit!*

He pulled the sack all the way back to where he had skinned the pythons. After dropping it to the ground, he sat down to catch his breath. Once he was breathing normal again, Tommy felt around with his hands until he located the huge tree he had used to tie off his double-hook rig that held the carcass while he skinned the snake.

Leaning back against the gumbo-limbo tree, Tommy's thoughts were about the darkness he was now trapped in. *Them damn carcasses might draw anything; bear, panther, crocodile, or even s'more big pythons.* He had shoved the half-full bottle of Jack Daniels down in with the snakeskins, so he felt his way back across the shell mound until he found it. He tugged it along until he bumped into the tree again. *At least I can have m'self a shot'r two of nerve medicine till morning comes.*

With the bottle in his hand, he turned his back to the tree and sat down. Leaning back, he thought, *Somebody's messin with me.*

Tommy's lips were wrapped around Jack's neck as he took a long pull. With the bottle still bottom-side up, a noise caused him to get splashed with whiskey when his head jerked toward the sound.

~ O ~

State Representative, Janssen Hilo Grundik, walked into the State Capitol Lounge, a top watering hole for many of North Florida's policy-makers, political movers and shakers, Ponzi scheme masters, and the slimy vermin that thrives amongst the lot of them. It was only five short blocks from the Florida State Capitol Building, but was a million miles from where the owner, Percy Griffith, was born on a sheep station in Northern Territory, Australia.

Percy arrived in Florida for his first vacation ever, which was also his first trip out of Australia. Percy was thirty when he arrived in 2010 with twenty thousand USA dollars in a money belt around his slim waist, and a cool two million in an Australian bank.

At 15, Percy had concluded that his future was going to be bleak if he remained on a small outback sheep ranch. He said goodbye to his mother, and told her to tell his father, if he ever returns, "he can kiss my ass." Percy had arranged a ride with the ranch cook that was driving to Perth to pick up supplies and visit his folks.

A few days later, he was heading toward the Sydney skyline with two young college boys heading back to school. Before checking in at their dormitory, the two boys took Percy to Kings Cross, Sydney's version of Greenwich Village in the Big Apple.

Standing 6 foot 3 inches on bare feet and weighing in at 230 pounds of pure muscle, young Percy was soon approached by a gorgeous 20-year-old hooker named, Ruby.

By the time Percy was 20, he had one dozen very good-looking hookers working for him. They were all being supervised by Ruby, who now only worked when a real, cash carrying, high roller hit the King's Cross area, and was willing to part with some serious money.

At 25, Percy and Ruby owned the best bar and brothel in King's Cross, the infamous Rainbows' End. He knew which politicians he should get acquainted with on a first name basis, and she knew how to make all of them keep coming back for more.

On Percy's 29th birthday, he met a nightclub owner he liked from Tallahassee, Florida during his huge birthday bash at The Rainbows' End. By the time that club owner left Sydney, Percy had already made up his mind. He would move to America and try his luck with the Yanks. "They are the horniest buncha blokes I've ever met," he said to Ruby. His constant smile widened, "I reckon they'd swap a new paid off Ford Mustang for one night in that warm hairy hole of yours, Ruby."

Ruby had kept her body in tip-top shape, and a daily facial kept her looking young and gorgeous. She grinned wide at Percy, " 'Ow in 'ell do y'reckon I got that bloody Cadillac I drive, mate?"

"Oh krikey," Percy wailed with a smile, "y'sent one o' me Yank customers 'ome walkin' wi' an empty rucksack, y'did, eh?"

"Nope," Ruby chided, "sent the bloke 'ome wi' a 'uge smile on 'is puss, an a fine bloody basket full o' memories 'e will n'er forget."

Percy's smile was wide as he turned back toward her, "A bleedin Florence Nightingale I reckon y'be, lass."

After landing in Tallahassee, Percy rented a car at Avis and then he got directions to his new American friend's club. A month later, he paid the man one million dollars for the building, property, contents, and business. Renovations cost him another half million, but he felt certain he would make a fortune once he located enough good looking, high-end hookers to service the state politicians.

He did, and several years later, it was through these very same politicians that sought the services of his extremely discreet ladies. Percy began building files on the men that could eventually help him reach his goals.

Two very powerful men in particular were the key to Percy accumulating the fortune that he would require in order to retire and live the plush life of ease to which he had become accustomed.

Livingston Cardiff Maule was the key, and Senator Bradley Ule Pierpont was the man who could turn that key for Percy.

~ O ~

"Senator Pierpont," Livingston Maule said softly, as he leaned a bit forward, "I can mobilize one hundred giant earth haulers, and have them heading toward those worthless damn Everglades to begin filling it, once you give Percy the word." He then sat back and puffed on his signature Jose Marti.

"Livingston," the senator said, "I have everything in place," he pursed his lips and took a deep breath, "with one exception." He picked up his Alexander brandy cocktail and took a sip while looking over the edge of the tulip-stem glass, directly at Livingston Hewlett Maule. He remained silent a moment as he thought about what he should say. "The governor," he said, almost in a whisper to keep nearby unwanted ears from hearing, "has a young friend down in Everglades City; well, not actually a friend, the governor's father was a close friend of this young mans' father. "Anyway, the governor has a soft spot where that kid is concerned, because he still credits the young guy's dead father for getting his own father into the governor's chair, and paving the way for his own ascent into that very same chair."

Senator Pierpont picked up his cocktail and leaned back in the plush leather chair. After a lengthy pause to think about this scheme that, if it was handled right, would make them all very wealthy, or, as was the case, wealthier. Senator Pierpont leaned forward and spoke softly. "I know Governor Skip Halsey quite well, so I'll talk to him and see if we can't come up with a solution that will benefit all of us." He glanced at both men, "Including the State of Florida."

The Senator dialed Livingston's office number, and then flipped it on speaker. When his secretary answered, he gave her his name and number and said, "Please have Livingston call me at his earliest opportunity."

The senator's cell phone vibrated an hour later. He was still at the bar, so he pulled it out of the small holster fastened to his belt, after leaning over to lift his huge belly. "Bradley, here."

"Livingston, Bradley. What's up?"

"I need to talk with you Livingston; can you stop by the Capitol Lounge for a drink?"

Rick Magers

"Percy there today?"

"Yeah, I was just talking to him."

"Gonna take me an hour to get free, so how about asking him if Lilly can spend the weekend with me in Bimini."

"Hang on a minute, he's heading this way, I'll ask him." A moment later, he had the cell phone back on his flabby red ear. "Livingston?"

"Yeah, Brad."

"Percy said she'll be here in an hour with her bag packed." He could hear the joy in Livingston's voice.

"Oh boy, Brad, that's great. I'll see you in about forty-five minutes. Is this gonna take long?"

"Five minutes."

"BCNU." He disconnected.

Half an hour later, Lilly walked in with her overnight bag hanging from her shoulder. "Hi Senator Bradley." Her soft, sweet, nineteen year old voice filled his head with daydreams as she walked past.

*Goddamnit, I wish t'hell Martha would take a trip out to California to visit her folks.* He could still see Lilly's cute little ass swinging back and forth, as she walked to the end of the hallway and tapped on Percy's office door. *God, what I could do during two hours between the sheets with that.*

The senator was still having X-rated daydreams about *his* Lilly when Livingston Cardiff Maul climbed up on the stool next to him. "So, what's cooking, Brad?"

"The goddamn governor sounds like he is gonna stick by that goofy goddamn kid with the sillyass goddamm giant swamp buggy that I told you about."

After a long pause to consider all of the possibilities, Livingston said softly, "I think it's time for us to hear a little more of what Percy was talking about, day before yesterday, but for now, Lilly and I are going to have a fun weekend in Bimini."

"Going in one of your planes?"

"Yep." He emptied his glass and climbed off the stool, "she really loves landing in the water, so I'm taking the Widgeon again."

~ O ~

Jintan's jet landed at the Barranquilla, Colombia Airport before Amad's Learjet landed at Miami International. He made his way to the private hanger where the Grumman Mallard seaplane was sitting behind mammoth closed doors. After parking his rental car, he opened his cell phone and hit number three, twice. Moments later, a voice asked in Spanish who it was.

Jintan answered in Spanish, "The plumber, I'm here to fix your toilet."

Rick Magers

A huge black man who had already recognized Jintan through the brass peephole opened the door. If he had answered 'the plumber, I'm here to fix your sink', the man inside would have known that Jintan was being held as a hostage. They would have been able to call one of their snipers outside to take the man out.

He stepped inside and was pleased to see that several men were wearing their police uniforms, complete with sidearm. Six other men were seated in strategic positions, and each was holding an AK-47 machinegun.

He was aware Amad had met with the mayor of Barranquilla, also a devout Muslim, and had secured a group of Muslim police officers from his city force. The only duty they had until the plane was in the air was to guard the seaplane and the men inside the hanger. A donation of half a million American dollars was left with the mayor to be used at his own discretion.

~ O ~

Jake Brown's lawyer, Isaac B. Stein, scheduled a meeting with the Everglades City Council, and Mayor Gerald Proctor.

Isaac Stein was a very successful lawyer whose Marco Island law firm had grown from just him and his one associate in 2013 to sixteen competent lawyers. They had defended clients accused of everything from murder to grand larceny and had never lost a case.

Isaac Stein had his personal policy spelled out on a huge, round brass plaque on the front of his three-story building: Be The Best—Hire The Best.

Guinevere Brown sat in the hall while her husband, Jake, and his attorney met with city officials to determine if he would be allowed to continue using Everglades City as the base of his Everglades walking tour.

Guinevere was not a nervous person, but now found she was antsy and for the first time she was nibbling at her fingernails. *Lord,* she thought, *Jake dreamed of this business for years and has worked so hard to make it a success.* She squeezed her eyes together tightly to keep tears from starting. *Please Lord, help him through this. We want to raise our children here in Everglades City. We've given ten percent of everything we have earned to our church ever since we married, and will continue to whether or not he gets through this. Thanks for listening, Lord. I will let you get on back now to Your more important business.*

One hour after sitting down, Guinevere heard the big door open, and saw her smiling husband walking toward her shaking fists of victory above his head.

"Everything's okay, darlin. Mister Stein explained a few little-known laws governing small, independently owned businesses in rural districts. I also agreed to hire an armed person to walk at the tail end of my tour to insure that this does not happen again. My five-hundred thousand dollar liability policy is enough, but I'm certain my premium will go up." He smiled and hugged her, "I am so happy to still have a business here in Everglades."

"Take time to thank Him." She pointed up.

"Been talking to Him for me, huh?"

"Yep."

"A prayer asking for divine help," Isaac said with a wide grin, "never hurts."

Guinevere hugged the short, kinky-haired lawyer, "I hope you'll stop by one day and have a big ole stone crab dinner with us, Mister Stein."

"You can count on that, Missus Brown, because I love fresh stone crabs." He shook Jake's hand. "Gotta get back to work, now. Good luck with your walking tour, Jake.

~ O ~

Percy Stan Griffith left Tallahassee a few days after his meeting with Senator Bradley Pierpont, and the land developer, Livingston Cardiff Maule.

The two men were used to dealing with men that took care of problems their own way. After listening to the two men explain in greater detail than they had at their first meeting with Percy, what he said in reply did not in the least surprise them.

Rick Magers

"Gentlemen, I've been dealing with men like this poor silly twit that lives in a bloody swamp truck since I was big enough to hold and fire a pistol, and that was before I left me teens." Percy looked hard at the senator, and then at Livingston. "Gentlemen, I approach everything like it's a business, and my business is to make money. I'll cut through the bullshit so we can get back to our individual business problems. The minute you give me a brown bag or a lunch tin with two hundred thousand dollars in it, I reckon your problems with the swamp boy are bloody well history." Again, he looked hard at the two men.

"I like your style, Percy, I'll be right back." Livingston stood and left the room.

"Looks like you were right about this bloke, Senator, 'e knows what 'e wants and is willing to pay for it."

"Percy, how about buzzing the bartender to send us a jug of good scotch to seal this deal with."

The cocktail hostess and Livingston arrived at the same time; her with the booze, and him with a brown bag containing two hundred thousand dollars.

For the five hundred mile trip to Everglades City, Percy chose his new Dodge sedan, which was registered in Georgia and had Georgia tags.

Rick Magers

220

Uninvited

He had already called a man he knew in Naples that he could trust, and left a message. "Trotsky, Percy, call me." He closed his cell phone and waited for the Russian to call from a safe pay phone, or an unregistered cell phone. He always destroyed the phone once his business was completed.

The phone beeped. "Got an easy job for you. I'll stop by with ten big ones if you get it to me in time." He gave him Abner Brown's name and description, and told him he wanted to know where he kept his swamp buggy and airboat, and any other information he could get about the guy. "Use your Russian charm so you don't make those local folks suspicious. I'll get a local room, so call me as soon as you have something."

~ O ~

Tommy Seegar took a deep breath, and slowly lowered the bottle of Jack Daniels and screwed the top back on. Silently leaning back against the big gumbo-limbo tree's trunk, he carefully placed Jack against the tree, and then lifted his butt so he could ease his knife from the leather sheath.

He remained motionless for half an hour, still holding the razor sharp hunting knife, blade up. *Som'n is movin' around out there, and it ain't far away.*

Rick Magers

His heart thundered like never before as his eyes did their best to penetrate the darkness. Both of his legs were aching and his back felt as though there were baseball size nodules on the tree where his back was.

*Holy shit, that sonuvabitch, whatever the hell it is, ain't far away now.* His eyes were still trying desperately to find whatever it was creeping toward him. *Lord, in all of my thirty-three years I ain't done a whole lot of church goin, but by Christ, if you'll juss git me outa this mess, I'll darn sure be there ever Sunday fer the rest of my life. An I promise not to steal no more crabs or crawfish or snakes or anything. Lord, I ain't done a bunch of church work, but by Christ, if you'll get me out of this mess, I'll darn sure be there ever dern time You need me fer the rest of my life. An I promise not to ever steal no more anything. You will have a new Christian that doesn't drink likker or even beer, and there won't be no more cussin and chasin wild wimmin. Lord please help me now and I'll work hard fer You the rest of my life.* He sat there next to the gumbo-limbo, silently thinking. *I'm juss thirty-three, same as Your son, Jesus, was when them damn Italians killed him, and that's too young to die.*

For fifteen frightening nightmare minutes, there were no sounds whatsoever. *Ain't heard nothin in quite a while.* It was as if every living thing but Tommy had deserted the area. *By golly, Lord, I reckon you've come to this ole sinner's aid, and I promise You that I'll do juss what I said I would.* His heart had stopped beating so violently,

Rick Magers

and he was not hearing a thing. He noticed the slight light when thick overhead clouds opened a small spot for starlight to cast a small glow where he sat shivering inside. He tilted his head up and looked at the stars. *A sign. . . oh, thank You dear Jesus, oh dear Lord, I thank You. I'll be the best Christian that you ever knew.* Tommy's face had burst open with a smile.

A pair of eyes that saw better at night than any night-vision device that man had yet been created, saw a flashing beacon of white as Tommy looked up and exposed the Adam's apple section of his white neck.

The prehistoric beast homed in on the white beacon at the same moment that Tommy looked down. The huge open jaws of the python sunk its needle teeth into both ears and the jaw of its prey.

Tommy's screams were muffled by the beast's mouth as it thrashed around getting the prey into position. Only a moment later, the first coil was around its prey, and was squeezing the life from it. Two more blurs and a second and then a third coil were rapidly constricting until there was no air in the animal's lungs—it was dead.

Three days later, when Abner Brown checked the same hammock where he had seen Tommy skinning pythons, he found a knife. *Yep, that's damn sure Tommy's hunting knife.* He held it in his gloved hand for only a moment looking at the carefully sharpened edge before

Rick Magers

throwing the knife as far out into the swamp as he could. Brushing his leather gloves together, he spotted a gunnysack. As he lifted it up a half-full bottle of Jack Daniels No. 7 fell out. He checked the sack but found nothing else.

After pouring the contents of the bottle into the shell mound, Abner returned it to the sack and tossed it into the swamp. *Looks like we've got one less thief to put up with.*

~ O ~

**P**ercy remained very low key during the first few days. He rented a room for a week and paid cash at the old refurbished Everglades City Motel. Once his clothes were hanging in the closet he got back into his Dodge and removed the latex gloves. Percy then drove around the area familiarizing himself with the layout of the streets. He wanted to be sure there were no dead ends or streets under construction that could prevent him from getting out of town in a hurry if necessary. *I learned a good lesson,* he thought, *in Jacksonville last year when I whacked that guy for my lawyer. Nobody was chasing me, but there it was right in front of my damn car, a goddamn dead end street with no sign where I entered.*

He followed the Barron River south toward the town of Chokoloskee. When he realized that he was west of the road that would put him on the causeway, Percy turned left toward the towers in the city circle. There was not a car behind him, so he stopped to make a mental note before turning south to go across the causeway and on to Chokoloskee. *The only road that has no stop signs is the one straight ahead of me. It turns north at that restaurant;* he picked up his small notebook and silently read his notes, *The Seafood Junction. That's the road I came in here on, State Road Twenty-nine. About four miles to Tamiami Trail then cross it and stay on twenty-nine until I get up onto Interstate Seventy-Five heading toward Tampa.*

His second day in the area, Percy slowly drove on through the small fisherman's village again, and then headed back across the causeway. *Oughta hear from Trotsky soon, so I'm gonna stay low-key and unrecognizable.* Slowly driving through the main sections of Everglades City, he had the basic layout of the small town in his memory.

Percy stopped at the small food market, and bought a half-gallon of milk, a box of Wheaties, his favorite cereal, sugar, a small jar of Nescafe, a loaf of bread, and two cans of Spam. After grabbing Styrofoam bowls and cups, he checked out and headed toward the motel. *Wish I had checked out the bloody fridge,* he thought, *to be certain that it works.* He laughed as he backed out, *if it doesn't I'll just eat the lot n' get more tomorrow.*

The small fridge worked fine, and Percy enjoyed the first can of Spam as sandwiches. He picked up the empty can and read the label. *"With jalapenos." Dunno what the 'ell a bloody jalapenos is, but it*

Rick Magers

*'as a nice zip to it.* He took a big bite of sandwich, *the Spam is delicious right outa the bloody tin, but that stuff actually makes it better. Gonna 'afta find out where I can buy a jar of it. Bet it would be tasty spread on a sardine sandwich.*

He did not watch television, so after a hot shower and a shave, Percy looked over the dozen or so books resting on a bookshelf. Finally choosing Vince Flynn' first novel, Kill Shot, he settled back into the pillows that he stacked on the bed against the headboard and began reading.

Halfway through the book, he fixed another coffee. Two spoons of sugar followed a huge tablespoon of Nescafe before shoving the cup into the microwave. At 2 o'clock in the morning, he put the book back on the shelf, and stretched out on the bed. *By Jesus,* he thought as the scenes ran through his head again, *that Mitch Rapp guy is one serious bad ass. I gotta stop by a bookstore and see if that guy wrote any more with Rapp as the main character.*

The following day, Percy drove around the small town again, as though he was a typical Georgia tourist looking the place over. He drove slowly back toward the road connecting Everglades City to Chokoloskee, one of the Ten Thousand Islands prior to the causeway being built back in the 50s. Percy spotted a skinny man up ahead walking along on the side of the road, flinging his arms back and forth as though they had just been lubricated.

Rick Magers

As a very young boy, Percy had developed the ability to size up a person by their body language, and several other traits that ordinary people usually missed.

The man walking ahead of him was Morton Gomez. Morton was a man that boasted about never having a regular full time job in his life. "Nossir, I'm a free man who sleeps when I want to, drink when I want to and work when I want to. Work is for men what ain't got sense enough to git along good, day by day, without doin too much of it."

Morton always managed somehow, but nobody knew exactly how, to not only get enough to eat every day, but also get enough wine, whisky, or beer to never quite sober up.

Percy eased his car up slowly beside Morton Gomez, and the moment he saw the man turn toward him, when window and tire noise alerted him that he had company, he felt certain this man would know everything that went on in the two small towns. After running the window down, Percy said, "G'day mate," with a friendly smile and a thick catchy accent, "I'm 'oping you can 'elp me locate someone, sir."

The 'sir' usually worked wonders—it did this time too. "I sure would like to try, but a pal over yonder," he pointed at a group of houses, "has a six-pack he wants to share with me if I'll tell him where the bigger stone crabs are hiding."

Percy's friendly smile was still there, even though he thought, *conniving asshole.* "Well, neighbor, 'ow about we pick up a couple of cold six-packs that you can carry wi' you when I bring you back to your pal's place. In the meantime, I'll describe the man that I've been trying to meet up with since yesterday. If you can't 'elp me locate 'im, I'll just carry you back 'ere wi' the beer, and will keep lookin for him m'self."

"Sure thing," a grinning Morton said, as he pushed open the door and climbed in. "Let's head to the Kangaroo in Everglades, while you tell me who yer lookin for."

"Well mate," Percy said in his heavy Australian accent, as he turned left and headed back north across the causeway, "my boss up in Atlanta 'eard about a fella that lives around 'ere somewhere on a 'uge swamp buggy. The guy kills them big snakes that are eating all of the small animals in the Everglades." He turned toward his passenger, "My boss makes movies for television, and 'e thinks one about this bloke would sell. This swamp fella will make a lotta money if I can find 'im."

Percy paused briefly to let what he had just said sink in. When Morton turned to look at Percy, he added, "I reckon my boss would like to 'ave a local bloke like you in the movie, too."

A slight pause, until Morton finally spoke. "That has gotta be Abner that your boss man is talkin about, Abner Brown. He don't live on his swamp buggy, but he stays on it a long time when he's out there in the Glades. Got hisself a big ole round building where he lives n' keeps his buggy. Got him a right nice little room in it too, with a shitter, shower, an everthang. Hardly ever comes to town here. I was out there once a while back when he hired me to cut down some trees." He turned to look at Percy again, "I was a good sawyer, back when I was a young feller, an he knowed it, so he come a'lookin fer me, especialificlee."

"Well darn," Percy said with the same plastic smile on his face, "I sure made a smart move when I stopped to talk to you, uh, what's your name?"

"Morton Gomez, an you kin always find me around here in Everglades or over on Chokoloskee." He turned his unwashed, tremor-ridden head toward Percy, "I ain't got no regler place to live at, but you kin axe anyone on the waterfront where I am, an they'll tell ya." His green hairy smile made Percy's stomach tremble.

Morton winked before talking again, "Like ifn thet er boss of yourn wants me t'be in thet mooovy, too."

"Oh, I'm sure 'e will, Morton, but first you've gotta tell me 'ow I can find this place where Abner keeps 'is swamp buggy. I 'afta talk wi' 'im about the film offer that my boss wants me to explain."

"Ain't no problem atol findin it," Morton said as they slowly made their way across the causeway. "Juss go on across the Trail until you come to the big highway what you kin drive under, but don't go thet far. Turn aroun' an head back t'ards the way y'come.

Rick Magers

Drive slow juss a bit, mebbe a half mile or not even thet much, an when y'see up ahead on the right, a single, big ole gumbo-limbo tree, look fer a small road, juss past it. Y'gotta go way on  down thet road, mmmmm, mebbe five miles an there it is, right next to the swamp, a big ole roun building; well not really roun, cause it looks like a big ole iron culvert pipe what was cut smack in half longways."

*Hmmmmm,* Percy thought while Morton tried to get a cigarette lit with his shaky hands, *that bugger has a Quonset hut back there in the woods, and not very far from Interstate Seventy-five.* A wicked smile flashed across his face, *This is going to be easier that I thought.*

~ *Yeah, right!* ~

~ O ~

Jintan watched closely as the ten boxes, five big equipment and five cocaine, were being were loaded aboard the seaplane. He had earlier ordered his five men who were going with them to Florida, to bring all ten boxes to the hanger. The youngest was forty, and all were Iranians, who had been trained as terrorists while still in their teens.

Only Jintan and Amad knew what all of the boxes contained. Five contained advanced-technology timers and detonating devices. Once they were married to the five nuclear bombs that were now on location in Miami, New York City, Chicago, San Francisco, and Los Angeles, each one would cause more damage and more deaths than the attack on the twin towers by their martyr, Osama Bin Laden.

Those five and five similar looking boxes containing the cocaine were loaded and secured in place by a cargo net.

Both pilots arrived and informed Jintan that to arrive on time in the Everglades, they must be airborne in one hour.

Everyone, including the pilots, machinegun men, and the police were from Iran. Prayer rugs were spread out on the concrete floor of the hanger, and fifteen minutes of prayer commenced.

A silent, somber group entered the plane a short time later and secured themselves while the pilot and co-pilot went through their pre-flight checklist.

Twenty minutes later, the Grumman Mallard's two huge, 600 hp, Pratt & Whitney, radial engines pulled the seaplane out of the hanger and toward their designated runway. A few minutes later, Jintan watched as the huge seaplane began the climb to altitude. He turned away and headed toward the executive terminal where a Lear Jet, which he had leased for a return trip to Miami, waited.

~ O ~

**A**bner brought the huge Swamp Castle to a stop near a small hammock. After killing the engine, he turned to Burt. "I ain't told you about this experiment yet, because I'm still trying to iron all of the kinks out." He glanced at Burt, who just shrugged his shoulders. "I built a re-bar cage big enough to hold a big female python, and then carried it here on the Swamp Castle and rigged a pulley on a big cypress. I then used half-inch trap rope and my big hydraulic pinch-disc to drag it into place. I put a female in it about the time you arrived and she shoulda come into heat by now. My scientist pal that works for the zoo in Miami checked her out and said she has not been exposed to a male yet, so she oughta be ready to have her first batch of eggs. And if that already happened, then it should have drawn a bunch of males straight to her."

"Sounds like a right good idea," Burt said. "Gonna use the pet python on 'em if they're there?"

"Nope, because if there happened to be five or six at the cage, the noise that pistol makes would cause all but a couple to haul ass before I could shoot 'em, and I don't wanna just wound one. It might lie out there in the darn swamp somewhere suffering for a long time until he died and I damn sure don't want that on my conscience."

Burt's eyebrows scrunched down and his lips twisted sideways. Finally he asked, "Then how are you gonna get 'em all?"

Rick Magers

Abner got down on his knees and pulled a leather case from beneath his bunk. "A good friend loaned me his sniper rifle. It has a sound suppressor that makes it sound like a pellet gun, and a scope like none I've ever seen."

Burt watched while Abner assembled the weapon. He was amazed how quickly the man put the gun together and attached the silencer and scope, but he said nothing.

Abner held out the clip for Burt to see before inserting it. "Seven point six-two NATO rounds." He handed the weapon to his friend, "Take a look through this scope, Burt."

Burt lifted the rifle and was amazed how light it was, and then he made a comment about the weight.

"Modern material, Burt." Abner said, she's light as a feather and tough as a gator's hide." Burt took the gun and pointed at a very small attachment at the front of the stock. "That, Abner said, "adjusts for distance, wind, and altitude. When a red blip in the scope turns green, all y'gotta do is pull the trigger."

Burt cautiously followed Abner through the dense bush of the small hammock. Ten minutes later, they arrived at the downwind edge of a very small clearing, which had obviously been created a short time earlier.

*Wow!* Burt's eyes were riveted to the python that was coiled on top of the six-foot square trap. He counted five more big pythons lying close to the eighteen-inch high cage, and assumed there were more on the far side that neither man could see.

He held his breath as Abner raised the rifle. All Burt heard was six deep phuwack, phuwack, sounds. After Abner inserted a full clip into the rifle, they remained in the brush at the edge of the clearing for five minutes.

Seeing no movement, Abner handed the rifle to Burt, and pulled his Colt Python out of the holster and opened the cylinder. When he closed it and moved toward the trap, Burt held the barrel straight up and followed. He had seen his friend insert a new clip and pull the lever back enough to be sure a cartridge was in the chamber. *All I hafta do,* he thought, *is flip the safety off like he showed me, and she's ready to fire.*

Abner put a bullet in the head of the six huge snakes. "I thought I had missed that first shot at the one on top of the cage, but I kept putting the cross-hairs on a new one." He pointed at a hole just behind the eye and up a little. "I must have severed the spinal cord of the one on top."

He filled the cylinder with new cartridges and put the Colt Python back in the holster. Grinning at Burt, he said, "Looks like the cage paid for itself today, huh?"

"Yep, and it looks like you have another helper on the payroll." Burt nodded at the female inside the trap.

"You're right." He leaned down toward the female snake in the trap, which had not moved during the brief commotion. "I'll bring you a nice big groundhog or som'n when I come back, darlin." He turned to Burt, "I reckon we better get started on these snakes. Ain't showed you my skinner yet, have I?"

"Nope."

"That engineer pal I told you about, who designed and built most of the Swamp Castle for me, designed the drag apparatus that I use to pull the snakes out with, and the skinner too."

~ O ~

Samson Blackraven saw the red light on his phone panel blink.

He knew it was Orlando Julio Carvojol, on the floor above in NSA communications. O J, as all of the staff on each floor referred to the native Colombian, had been with the CIA for over 20 years. He was raised in America, and retired from the Army after serving twenty years in MI wearing an eagle on his broad shoulders.

Samson pressed the big white button to engage the desk speaker in front of him, "What's up, O J?"

"The boat's in the sky with an ETA of midnight."

"Gracious, amigo."

Samson hit the blue button on the NORAD panel and was immediately connected to General Masterson. "Hello Samson, the flying boat in the air?"

"Yessir, General, so I've already bumped us up to Operation Shine."

"Good! SEAL teams seven and eight are in the swamp now and setting up. The National Park Service has put ten airboats around the perimeter a mile from center. They are keeping all traffic out by stating that it is a mock military war games area. No airboats, canoes, kayaks, or swamp buggies will be allowed in. All available satellites will be monitoring activity in the red zone until all targets are either dead or captured. Keep me informed of any changes, Samson. Over and out."

Samson pressed the button that put him in direct contact, after being funneled through his communication officer's filter, with the commanding officer of SEAL teams 7 and 8. Less than five seconds later, a very deep voice answered, "Captain MacGregor here, sir."

Samson Blackraven, here, captain. Was your daddy Ian James MacGregor?"

"Yessir."

"I worked with him, captain. He is a warrior of the highest order. How's he doing?"

"Fit as a fiddle, enjoying himself as a hunter of edible animals now."

"That's really good news t'hear, captain. What you n' I must do, now that the enemy is in the air and heading this way, is be very certain we are all on the same page." He paused a moment.

"Very good, sir."

"Okay, captain. Your men driving the airboats will be ready, once the plane starts moving and the pilots are occupied with getting the plane airborne, to kill the men who came aboard with the packages, point blank, and with no hesitation."

"Yessir, we have practiced that scenario many times during this past week, and have it down pat. Those five men all have seen heavy combat and understand that this mission might change the history of the United States of America, if everything isn't done right."

"Good, captain, that is why this operation demanded a group of hand-picked professional soldiers. Now, we have installed a beacon that only your SEAL teams can see, and two backups, to lead you to the drop-off point. The airboat operators have practiced with them, I assume."

"Yessir, they have, and will be able to run straight to the drop-off point, where SEAL team eight is setting up as we speak."

"Very good. And they know that only our undercover man will be wearing painted clothing observable through SEAL team night-vision gear only."

"Yessir, they do. That'll be Jerome, correct?"

"Yes, and in the event that some unknown situation pops its ugly head up and a shootout occurs...Samson paused.

"Our best two handheld missile-men," the captain continued, "will have their night-vision scope following the plane from touchdown to liftoff."

"Excellent, Captain MacGregor. As soon as you give us the signal that all enemy are either dead of subdued, I will send in the helicopters to light up the place like a swamp version of Coney Island, and the ground troops I have waiting in the wings will be there in minutes. You have questions, captain?"

"Nossir, we're ready."

"Good luck and God Bless. Over and standing by."

~ O ~

Abner and Engelbert were able to pull four of the five pythons through the marsh to the swamp buggy. They had to work together on the big one that was lying on top of the cage. "That sucker," Burt had said while cautiously making their way to the short wooden walkway where the Swamp Castle was parked, "didn't look like a big one while it was lying on top of the cage."

"Yeah," Abner agreed, "mebbe I shoulda used the hydraulic winch to drag these suckers out. When I first started messin with these pythons, I was surprised several times. I told Leon once that a snake we'd been watching was probably ten or eleven feet long." He grinned down at Burt from where he was unbolting the end of the skinner, "She was eighteen feet long when we straightened her out to measure."

"I can sure understand that. Betcha this one is close to that."

"Hmmm," Ab mused, "Fifteen, at least." He lowered the end of the skinning rig to Burt and had him support it until he could get down and fasten it.

The hydraulic pinch-head unit that could be rotated on the extendable swiveling boom from forty-five degrees up toward the rear, would pull a snake twenty-foot long or shorter snakes straight down, to skin them.

"Okay, Burt, just move back now and watch how easy it is to skin one with my pal's invention."

Burt watched as Abner cut off the head of the one he was talking about, that was on the trap and did not look so long, but it had measured fifteen feet three inches. Abner tossed the head in a wire basket, and then used his knife to work the skin back and open an area of meat a foot long. He then slid the adjustable, stainless steel circular blade, down over the python's headless carcass and locked it in place. After shoving the four inch long curved stainless pins that were attached to the heavy nylon rope in the pinch-head puller, into the meat, opposing each other, he bent down and adjusted a razor sharp stainless steel blade that would slice the belly skin as the carcass was pulled through the cutter. The entrails would then fall on the ground as the snake was pulled through. Abner held the rope to prevent it from slipping while the pinch-disc puller brought the meat through the skinner.

Several minutes later, they had a skin almost fifteen feet long lying at their feet, and a chunk of hanging meat that was as long.

"First thing we've gotta do," Abner said, "is chop the meat into sections and get 'em into the freezer. This is my own invention." He opened a tool bin and pulled out what looked like a huge set of hedge shears. "I was cutting the meat into chunks by hand, using a sharp knife and a hand saw, but knew there had to be a better way. I made one out of plywood and bolted it together to see if it would open enough to fit big snakes. It looked right, so I had this one made out of stainless steel, and as you're about to see, it works great."

Abner got the plastic tote-boxes down from where he had tied them. He placed one beneath the hanging meat, and then went to the rope that was hanging down from the pinch-head discs.

"C'mere Burt, and hold this while I get it out of the discs."

With Burt holding the end of the ¾-inch rope, he climbed up to the puller. "Okay, Burt, hold tight but give me slack when I ask for it so I can move the rope to a pulley I welded to the mast." With Burt holding it, he put the rope in the pulley. "Hold it now while I reverse these discs, and then you'll have the snake held tight in the pulley.

With Burt holding the rope, Ab climbed back down and opened the chopper so he could fit it around the snake. Before chopping off a section of meat, Abner eased the chopper ahead until the stainless steel measuring rod touched the end of the snake meat.

The blade easily sliced through the snake, and the section fell into the plastic tote-box. "Ease it down, Burt, as I move the box and whack off a chunk."

Three hours later the two men had hoisted the boxes of meat up to the main floor, and had stacked the sections in the freezer.

"I had those plastic sleeves made," Abner said, "so I'd be able to put the meat in before stacking them in the freezer and boy did it help." He grinned at Burt, "You shoulda seen what Leon and I went through to get those first few batches of snake meat back out of the freezer."

"Stuck together, huh?"

"Yeah, but Leon climbed down and got a big wide chisel and a stubby little hammer. After that, it wasn't so bad. He went with me the first trip after I had those sleeves made, and could not believe how easy it was to get 'em out of the freezer when we got home."

"Leon doesn't go with you every trip?"

"Nope, he is a bit too old to be humping like that on a regular basis," Ab looked at Burt and squinted his lips, "I sure wouldn't want him to know I said that, though. He's as tough as they come and as loyal a friend as any man ever had. I don't wanna shorten his time by putting him through those eighteen hour days, so I just take him along when I know it'll be a short day, and we'll be back in the barn in seven or eight hours."

"Have you got someone to go with you when you'll be out there, like you said, till you fill the freezer?"

"Yeah, but it took a while to find one. My nephew in Naples has been going with me the past two years. I call him and he's here in an hour or so, and he ain't missed a day yet."

"Man that must be some kind of record."

"I'm sure it is, Burt. He's always been a good, hard workin' kid, and I'm well aware that there ain't many like him these days, so I pay him good."

"Well," Burt said, "let's get those skins rolled up and see what the next stop has waitin for us."

~ O ~

Samson Blackraven listened to the real time, minute-by-minute surveillance of the Mallard Seaplane carrying the five devout terrorists and their deadly equipment…the course change is completed and Big Bird in now passing between Cuba and Jamaica… Agent Pablo Garcia was in the room with Chief, listening to the Central Intelligent Agency's Eye-in-the-Sky, which was a converted Hercules cargo airliner. The huge, high-altitude aircraft was carrying state-of-the-art equipment that was capable of automatically maintaining surveillance on a target through day/night telescopes. Two CIA satellites were also tracking Big Bird.

Samson and agent Garcia leaned forward each time a new message lit up the panel...Big Bird is now east of Cuba and heading toward Andros Island, Bahamas..."Just as I predicted. They will go down as though they're just another airplane landing at our AUTEC Submarine Base in West Andros, but, rather than landing, they will hold the plane at one hundred feet above the water and head straight for the Florida Keys, and probably go across between Marathon and Islamorada." He turned a grin toward Garcia, "The old drug smuggler's slick-trick back in the seventies and eighties, to stay below the radar."

"You'd think," Garcia, said, "they would know that we now have some very sophisticated equipment to keep people like them from slipping into America, unseen."

"Intelligence," Samson said, "is apparently not one of the traits that are demanded of the people who enroll in these terrorists' training schools in Iran."

"Must not be," Garcia said, shaking his head of coal black hair. The two covert operatives were drinking their umpteenth cup of coffee, when the speaker crackled… "Big Bird is now in the process of bleeding off altitude as they approach Andros."

"I had all the rain," Samson growled, "that Idaho would need to bring in a bumper crop of potatoes, the last two times the wife n' I decided to fly our Cessna 210 over to Nassau for a weekend, not to mention the gale force winds we had the entire way. These miserable pricks are enjoying a tail wind of ten knots and clear skies."

"One consolation, Chief, is they are not gonna have a nice flight home."

"Yeah," the huge Seminole said, "and their very own, not-so-dear **brother**," he empathized the word, "rigged up their plane with a bomb to go off between the Florida Keys and Cuba."

"I wonder," Garcia said with a slight smile, "if they'll still get the dozen virgins and ten cases of Bud Light, or whatever the hell they're promised when they become the martyr du jour."

"Hoo," Samson sputtered through a mouth full of hot coffee, "martyr du jour. Oh shit, I love it." After wiping up the coffee he spilled while laughing, he looked at his most trusted agent. "You don't pop up with many, Pablo, but when you do, they're beauties." He was wiping tears and coffee off his cheeks when the speaker came alive again… "Big Bird is now at one hundred feet altitude and heading straight toward a spot on the Overseas Highway just north of Marathon where there are few homes and no street lights."

"Well," Samson growled, "we oughta be able to wrap this up in the next few hours."

~ O ~

Abner was inside his Quonset hut working on a project on the Swamp Castle, when Percy stopped his car, half of a football field away. Abner's CD of George Jones was turned up a bit, so he could hear him sing, even when he was welding.

There were no windows or openings in the Quonset, except a few of the vents way up high. The only way in was through one of the steel roll-ups in each end, or a steel door in the eastern roll-up.

Leon was lying in bed reading Dark Caribbean, a novel by Rick Magers, based on a true story. A small speaker positioned above a bank of monitors sitting behind his corner desk, began making a noise like a cricket—berrrrrakkk, berrrrrakkk, berrrrrakkk. Quickly getting up, Leon turned down the cricket, and began to scan the twelve pictures on the big monitor. When he saw Percy's car in one, he pressed a button and the small image was transferred to another monitor. Now being able to see the vehicle better in full size on the second monitor, Leon flipped a switch, and suddenly he was looking at the rear of the car. Flipping another switch allowed him to manipulate the camera, only one of twelve small, professional, high-tech, solar recharged, clandestine spy cameras, which he had mounted in inconspicuous areas all along the road in, and on trees surrounding the Quonset.

Leon wrote the license plate number and state on the notepad in front of him, and entered it into a website he was given access to by old military friends. He quickly went to his bed and pulled out a black leather case, and placed it on the bed. A moment later, he was watching the car drive slowly in on Abner's road.

*I'll wait and see what this guy is up to before I buzz Ab. I don't want him comin out till I know what the hell's goin on.*

Leon moved the leather case to the desk, and while he watched the monitors, he began assembling the sniper rifle that he had used for twenty years as a U S Army Ranger Sniper until he retired.

A short time later, Leon watched as the man moved cautiously forward. When he spotted the pistol the man was holding as he fitted a silencer to the barrel, Leon opened the middle drawer and removed a small remote that would cause the lights inside the Quonset to dim and then flash on and off, to warn Abner. He pressed the button. *He'll slip out the emergency door with his night-vision glass on.*

Leon put a cartridge into the sniper rifle's chamber, and then slammed a full clip in, and put two more in the pockets of his cammys, which was all he wore when at home. He attached the night-vision scope, and then slipped out the rear door as silent as the mist that was now rolling in from the swamp.

~ O ~

**B**urt was sitting alone at the Chickee Bar in the Seafood Junction.

Maggie was setting up the bar for the afternoon crowd and chatting with Burt. "Where did you meet this young girl, Christina?" she asked.

"Orlo introduced her to me. He said her story, even without the python attack, would be good enough to go in a book.

Maggie stopped wiping the bar, "Python attack?" She asked Burt to tell her what happened.

"Well……………after Burt finished Christina's story, Maggie's mouth was hanging open and her head moved slowly back and forth as she said softly, "My God."

"Now here's the real kicker, Maggie," Burt grinned at her, then Said, "Christina is engaged to marry the first of those men, Angelo, that came running to rescue her daughter."

"Wow, what a great story, and with the exception of her young husband getting killed while diving, it has a nice happy ending."

"And get this, Maggie, Christina and Angelo are both from the same town, Limon, in Honduras. They played together as children, but Angelo moved to Immokalee as a teenager with his family."

Maggie softly whistled, "Burt, I'm certain you have enough material for a good book, but will your friend allow you to use it since he's paying your bills while you are here to write an article for his magazine?"

"I've already talked to him by phone. He said to stay here as long as it takes to accumulate enough for a book, and then once it's finished, we'll serialize it monthly in his magazine, and then he'll use his contacts in New York to have it published."

Maggie smiled, "Great, then I'll have you here with me for a while longer." She saw a man and woman enter the chickee, and put her bar cleaning rag down before turning to get their order. Two steps later she abruptly stopped and turned to look at Burt. "Huh?"

Burt whispered loudly, "I said, could you stand to have me around for the rest of your life?" His face broke open in a wide mix of happiness and expectation.

~ O ~

**W**alking with her young daughter, Angelina, along the narrow road in Everglades City that followed the Barron River, Christina mentally reminisced about the day two years previously when Mr. & Mrs. Grayson's generousity changed her and Angelina's life.

Rick Magers

She smiled watching Angelina skip along in the grass bordering the road. Across the narrow road was a row of commercial fishing boats that men were cleaning after a day at sea pulling stone crab traps.

Several were from Guatamala and Honduras, while others were Mexicans. They were all used to seeing the young woman and the small girl walking along the road near the boats they worked on. Some that had spoken to her and heard her speak in Spanish, greeted her in their language and waved with smiles at young Angelina, who was always thrilled to see people who were her friends, to wave at.

Christina saw something move beneath a huge ficus tree only two or three meters from her daughter. Her pace quickened, and a moment later she screamed when she saw what it was.

A huge python was slowly moving toward Angelina. The child was standing rigid like a statue with her eyes stretched wide and her mouth hanging open.

Christina's leg was raised in the position to sprint to help her daughter when she was suddenly bumped by someone and almost fell. Stumbling sideways she regained her balance and stared wide-eyed as a young Guademalan rushed past with his razor sharp machete held high.

Even though the machete bit deeply into the snake, right behind its head, the beast still flipped a coil around the diminutive young man.

"Angelo," another brown young man screamed as he too rushed past Christina with a huge, razor sharp machete held high. His blow hit just beyond the coil that was constricting his friend. Two more swift strokes that hit in the wound he had created caused the snake's head to flip violently side-to-side, as the young man continued hacking with his machete.

Christina had Angelina up in her arms and watched as a small army of Guatemalan, Honduran, and Mexican men rushed forward and began hacking on the beast. One went directly to the huge head and grabbed it with both hands. Still struggling, but weakened considerable, the python hissed loudly in the man's face as his friends removed the coil from Angelo's body.

By the time the boy was freed, and his friends had finally hacked the snake apart into two gruesome pieces; each about ten feet long, the head was still hissing. The others hacked away a yard or so from their friend who was still holding the monster's head. When it finally stopped hissing and went limp he let go and watched as what was left of the beast tried to writhe and wriggle toward the Barron River, a few yards away.

Christina knew all of the young men by sight, having walked past their fishing boats with Angelina many times since she had moved to Everglades City. She hugged each of them tight, thanking them all repeatedly.

Rick Magers

Angelina had her arms around her mother's neck and her legs wrapped around her tiny waist. She had stopped sobbing, but was still shivering as though the 80 degree weather had suddenly turned into a blizzard.

Angelo, the first man of the group of fishermen that rushed to prevent the snake from devouring Angelina, washed off his machete at a water spigot near his stone crab trap boat, and walked with Christina and her young daughter to their home. Half way to her house, Angelina loosened her grip on mama's neck. Her mother told her that the man walking with them saved her life by attacking the giant snake with his knife. After staring at Angelo for one long moment she asked in English, "Are you Superman?"

They both laughed, and the young man smiled wide, saying, "No Angelina, I am just a fisherman who cannot stand silent and watch a snake attack a little child."

By the time they reached her house, Christina and Angelina were both talking in English and Spanish with Angelo.

~ O ~

Morris Fent arrived at his old 12-foot wide mobile home in Lee Cypress in a bad mood. He spent the entire day on his stone crab trapping boat, once again trying to fix his haudraulic trap-puller.

Three days earlier, he had pulled only a few of his crab traps when his pinch-disc puller suddenly froze and would not turn forward or reverse. He and his hired man worked on it for an hour before giving up. He put Everglades City into the autopilot's GPS, and twisted the top off of a fresh bottle of cheap rum.

Once the boat was tied to the dock, they borrowed four quarts of hydraulic oil from another trapper. They poured the oil into the thirty-gallon recirculation tank, which was already close to empty. "Okay," Morris said, "we'll take it easy for a coupla days, and then head back out."

Three days later, Morris and his deck hand were aboard on the boat getting ready to head out. "Let's try that puller before we go," his deck hand said.

"Waste of goddamn time," Morris mumbled, "you's with me when I added oil, but if it'll shut ya up, Cap'n Fuh Quad, I'll go down in the engine room and engage the goddamn pump."

"Okay, Morris," his deckie yelled, "It's turning fine."

Morris was mumbling as he climbed up out of the engine room. "If you're through fukin' aroun, git them damn ropes off the pilings and let's git goin."

"Two goddamn hours running time t'git out here," he said to Hussein Phah Quaudi, "and the damn puller freezes up again." He emptied his glass and added fresh rum and another few chunks of ice from the Igloo strapped to the wall in the wheelhouse. After

Rick Magers

squeezing half of a Key Lime into the glass, Morris leaned back in the padded captain's chair, which Rita, his live-in girlfriend for the past nine years, bought him at a yardsale, a month earlier for his forty-second birthday.

"One goddamn line of twenty traps, and that fukin worthless piece o' shit trap puller quit agin."

He watched as Hussein drained his glass and plucked the bottle out of a PVC pipe that Morris had strapped to the wall after a full bottle of rum rolled over the edge of the dash and busted. "Take it easy on the rum, Fuh Quad, that's all we have."

Hussein's dark eyes scanned Morris as though he was someone who shouldn't be aboard. He poured a bit more rum in than he would have if Morris had kept his mouth shut, but that was a character flaw, and something he had never quite mastered, especially when he was drinking—which had become a 24/7 routine that Morris had mastered by his twentieth birthday, according to people that had known him that long. "I bought this one," Hussein mumbled as he returned the bottle to the plastic holder.

"Oh wow, Captain Fuh Quad. Who the hell do you think bought the last ten?"

"You the captain," Hussein said as his thin black eyes homed in on Morris' blood-streaked, milky grey eyes. "You're suppose to buy the stuff we need to stay out all day to get a good load of crabs." Lifting the glass to his lips he took a sip, and then added, "When you don't keep the motor and the other stuff on this boat fixed, we go on home with no pay check."

"How the hell am I supposed to know that the damn puller is gonna quit like that agin?" He drained his glass and got more ice before yanking the bottle out of the holder. "I reckon you've got the best damn job of any o' them Iran fukers in Naples where you live."

"I've been telling you that the puller tank needs fresh oil. We have been using the same stuff for years, and it's leaking out now. I been telling you that." He shook his head slowly then sipped his rum, "And you know that I am Iraqi, but was born in Naples and live with my aunt and uncle at Port of the Isles."

Morris had already started slurring his words. "Thirty and still living with your folks. Shit, I was out on my own when I was fifteen."

"Because," Hussein said softly, "they couldn't stand you any longer."

"Huh? What the goddamn fuck did you say, Captain Fuh Quad?"

"I said, when I get my law degree, you're going to be forced to sell this boat, because nobody but me will work for you."

"Hey, Fuh Quad, you can't get no law degree to be a lawyer on a computer."

Rick Magers

"You're wrong again, Captain Quigg." Hussein grit his pearl-white teeth, *there's only one fuckwad on this boat*. "About half," he continued, "of all the law degrees that are earned these days, are the result of the law cources offered online."

"Oh boy, home-made goddamn lawyers. As if there ain't enough half-ass legal-beagles out there already."

Hussein just shook his thick head of black kinky hair. "With all the fuckups out there these days," he paused while shaking his head, *like you and any kids you produce*, "we're going to need more lawyers."

"Whadaya do, Captain Fuh Quad? watch two years of Law and Order reruns, and send in some box tops of whoever sponsors the show, and then they mail you the degree so you can hang your shingle on the front of the Ted's Shed you're gonna be livin in?"

"You got it, and one of the first clients that I represent will probably be the guy who replaces me here, and kills you." Before Morris could think of a good reply, Hussein added, with a wide sarcastic smile on his handsome brown face, "I'm sure I can get him off scot-free."

When they reached Everglades City, Hussein had to get the boat backed into their slip on the Barron River. When the boat was secured, he helped Morris get off the boat and into his truck.

One of Hussein's friends followed him to Lee Cypress as he drove Morris home. He would drive Hussein back to his Harley

Davidson motorcycle, which was parked at Orlo's Triad restaurant.

Before leaving, Hussein explained what had happened, to Rita. "We'll get the puller working tomorrow," he raised his bushy black eyebrows, "or the next day, so we can get all of the traps pulled and baited."

Before he got into his friend's car, Rita whispered, "I want to see you tonight, Hussein, can I meet you in the bar at Port of the Isle?" She blinked her heavily coated eyelids and Wal-Mart plastic eye lashes.

"I wish I could, Rita, but unk and auntie are returning tonight from their vacation."

His friend grinned when Rita leaned down and put a huge smear of fire engine red lipstick all over Hussein's lips and surrounding face.

"I love you, Hussein, let's get together again, soon."

"I love you, too, Rita."

After they were back on highway 29, heading south towards Everglades City, his friend chuckled as Hussein was still trying to get all of the red lipstick wiped off his face. "Man, that is one good lookin hunk of woman, but she sure could sure use some modern makeup advice."

"All them Alabama gals're that way."

~ O ~

Rick Magers

The captain in the cockpit of the Mallard, Muhammad ibn Muquaffa, turned briefly to his co-pilot. "Shahid, we shall be going down in five minutes, and changing our altitude. It will appear on Florida and Cuba radar as if we are landing at AUTEC, the American submarine base on Andros Island. Have you been briefed about this?"

"Yessir, I have."

The young man had been sent to Colombia by his brother and sister, a few weeks prior to becoming martyrs. Al Qaeda had asked for a loving-couple-appearing pair of devout Muslim terrorists, and Shahid's siblings had both volunteered. Their mission for Allah was to carry a vest of plastique explosives, and enter the American military base/civilian employee compound, where they each had worked for the past two years as teachers to the young children belonging to the Americans that were currently holding positions in Iran.

These bargain basement terrorists were unaware that the revolutionary, high-tech explosive-detection technology had been created by the new, Anti-terrorism research-cell, located at NORAD in Cheyenne Mountain, Colorado. Both of Shahid's siblings calmly entered a very small building they were told was a new body-scanning area. It appeared, at least to them, to be just another checkpoint. They walked in and stood on the white square on the floor like they were told, as the door they had entered through closed.

Ten-feet-thick, reinforced walls, floor and ceiling, did what the engineers said it would. The gigantic explosion was barely heard as it vaporized the two zealots, the first of many to be sent to, what American technicians called, Martyrville.

Once the room was cleaned, it looked the same as it did prior to electronics activating the detonators attached to their vests. Word leaked within a year, and none of the locally hired help would enter what they called, "The boombox." Domestic help was imported from Honduras and Mexico. All Iranians, whether they were politicians, technicians, clergy, or anything else, went through 'The Boombox' or they stayed outside.

Shahid turned to Captain Muquaffa and spoke softly. "I was trained to fly close to water by Abu Shakur Jilani."

The captain smiled in the dark cabin and nodded his head, "I am happy to hear that, Shahid. He is the best of all the flight instructors that I have worked with."

After a full check of all his instruments, Captain Muquaffa said, "Okay Shahid, let's take her down to one hundred feet above the waves."

Once the Mallard was leveled out at 100 feet above a calm ocean, Shahid kept a steady grip on the controls, but said softly, "I praise Allah for allowing me to strike a blow against the infidels."

"Praise Allah," Captain Muquaffa whispered.

In a little over fifteen minutes, Captain Muquaffa spotted the lights of Marathon, in the Florida Keys, and took the controls. He eased the seaplane up to clear the power lines. The huge sea bird flew across A-1-A, the Overseas Highway that leads tourists through Key Largo and on into Key West. They flew across a section that had few homes or lights. In approximately fifty minutes she would be setting down in the Everglades between two flashing beacons.

~ O ~

Two young lovers, laying naked on a blanket, spread out on a cool summer beach between two sections of mangroves, heard a roar, and glanced up, but the bird had already passed. "I told my pal," the stoned boy said dreamily, "to fly his big mosquito-spray-plane right over us tonight when he goes to work. Won't be any mosquitos for a while, baby."

Her fifteen-year-old pupils were the size of pin-pricks as she tried to see her young lover. "Wow, Clyde, you are really a man to get to know, aincha?"

"Betcher ass, darlin. I don't wanna see nooooo skeeter bumps on that cute little ass of yours."

~ O ~

Amad reserved a small table in a dark secluded area at a new dinner house & lounge, Chez Casimeer, in North Naples, a short distance from Jerome's Seafood Market and Restaurant.

He sat in his brand new 2020 Cadillac el Diablo SUV in the passenger terminal of Naples Airport. When he spotted a Learjet on the final approach of landing, he looked at his gold watch. *Exactly when Jintan's plane should be landing, so it must be him.* He glanced at his wristwatch again.

Amad punched Jintan's cell phone number, and then lightly touched the Brain-Phone speaker implant in his earlobe. "Yes brother," he said in their language, which was picked up by the wireless mic in his gold tie-pin. "I am parked at the airport waiting for you. I will drive to the passenger arrivals area now." With his Brain Phone tucked away in the inner pocket of his $1800 Italian suit, Amad started the car and pulled slowly out.

Amad pulled ahead and Jintan climbed in. Before the two men were even out of the airport and onto US-41, the two CIA operatives that had followed Amad, were in the line of vehicles leaving the airport. They let two cars get in line between them and the two terrorists.

When the Cadillac turned left and headed north, there were four other cars, besides the one that had been following Amad earlier. They were on US-41 driving north too, and monitoring the wafer-thin tracking bug that a young agent had deftly placed on the top of Amad's car earlier, while at a stoplight impersonating a homeless person.

The 'homeless person' was picked up by the last CIA car following Amad and Jintan.

When the Cadillac turned into the parking lot of the new dinner house, the five CIA vehicles, each a different make and color, pulled into pre-determined observation spots. All of their moves had been established when their snoops learned of Amad's destination.

Three, male/female covert operative teams, casually entered, and were escorted to their reserved booths. Earlier in the day, a spook had entered Chez Casimeer, once Samson Blackraven knew which table Amad had reserved, to put a tiny wireless receiver-wafer on top of the table.

All three teams used the pre-determined signals to let the two agents that were sitting at the bar know that they were receiving perfect signals, and were recording all of the conversation between the two terrorists. One agent went to the men's room and sat on a commode while text messaging The Chief.

A moment later, he received a text message. 'Can hear them both as if they are in this room—Interpreter typing as they speak—Good work—Continue.'

The agent had loosened his tie, and unbuttoned the top two. After leaving the men's room, he stood near the end of the bar looking at his Smart Phone, smiling wide as though reading a text message. The three teams at their tables all saw that his tie was loosened, and knew that everything was going as planned.

~ O ~

**B**urt did not want Abner to think he was not anxious to go out with him, but he desperately wanted to spend more time with Maggie. Burt had pulled into Jim Webb's hardware store across the street and a ways north of Billy Potter's Seafood Junction, when Abner whipped in. With a big smile, Abner said, "Lynn just told me that you'll be staying a while longer."

"Yeah, my boss told me to stay until I have every bit of information I need to turn this into a book. I don't feel that a book, just about the snakes, as dangerous as they are, would be interesting enough on its own. What I plan to do now, is write about the people in Everglades City and Chokoloskee, and what their lives are like now, with all of the changes. Most of the ones who have spent their lives here have depended on the sea, in one way of another, to make their living, and now they must either leave or become involved with the tourist trade."

"I agree with ya, Burt. Most of the younger ones will be forced to move away to find jobs, but there'll always be those who ain't leavin', come hell or high water, because they just love it here. How long are you planning to stay?"

"Lynn said I can stay an additional three months, and that will be enough, to hopefully convince Maggie that I will be the best husband she'll ever get." Burt's grin was the widest that Abner had seen cross his face yet.

Abner chuckled, "From the way she looks at you, and acts when you're around, I think that's probably what she's already ciphered out for herself."

"Really?" Burt's voice squeaked a bit, it surprised him so much to hear that from Abner.

"Well," Abner drawled, "I damn sure ain't no match-maker, but from what Ginger tells me, I reckon Maggie is as interested in you as much as you are in her."

"Oh boy, Ab, you've made my day." He looked a bit alarmed then, "Uh, Ab, uh, I…

"Do not worry a bit, podnuh," he grinned, "I ain't givin' up no information. I just figgered you oughta know that she has a very high opinion of you."

"Thanks Ab. Hey, would me staying in for a while, screw things up for you?"

"No man, if you have things to do, git at it, and remember what I told you, I'm basically a one man band. If I really need some help, I won't hesitate to ask."

"Good deal, Ab, and if you ask, I'll drop everything and be ready to go."

"Okay, I'm going in here now n' get some Cool Seal to put on the top of Leon's place."

"Leaking?"

"Nah, he juss likes to add a coat ever coupla years, so it won't."

"What are you looking for in here?" He held the door open as Burt entered.

"I'm hoping they have a coffee maker, because that old Mister Coffee is screwing up half the time and I don't wanna ask Lynn for one."

"Forget it, Burt. A new one will be on the porch in the box this afternoon. Leon got a deal on six of 'em for twenty bucks about five years ago. The two we plugged in that same day are still working fine."

"Okay, thanks. Do I need to get some filters for it, cause I used the last one this morning."

"Nope, they're in the box. Just git some coffee."

"Okay, thanks. See you at Billy's place now n' then." Burt left the hardware smiling. *Boy, I'm glad Ab didn't need me to go with him. I'm dying to learn when Maggie gets a day off again.*

Abner put the Cool Seal on the passenger's side floor and fired up. As he headed out the road toward the Trail, he thought, *Boy, I'm glad Burt has other things to do. He's a really good hand to have along, but I'm much more comfortable all by m'self.*

~ O ~

**P**ercy heard the music coming from the huge Quonset. He turned off the lights and stopped. He pulled out the pistol from the right pocket of the old U S Army field jacket, and a moment later, he was attaching a silencer that he brought out of the left pocket.

Leon had created a standing platform at the base of a huge cypress tree, years earlier. He was now almost part of the tree as he adjusted the night-vision scope. He was still wondering who the man was and what was he doing here in the swamp at this time of night.

He stopped wondering when he saw the man attach a noise suppressor to the pistol he was carrying. *If he's a bill collector, he's the dumbest sonuvabitch they ever hired.* Leon put just enough pressure on the trigger to send the slug toward the man.

~ O ~

**M**aggie paused a moment after hearing what Burt had just said.

A look of disbelief quickly changed to pure joy. She went back quickly and whispered, "I would love it," and then continued toward her customers.

Later, when the bar was empty, except for an old man at the end, who was there almost every evening to drink the sun down, and often the moon up, Burt said, "I told my boss, Yan Shen, about you being an English Lit major, and graduating with a degree in that, plus accumulating enough credits to get a BA in creative writing." Wobbling his eyesbrows, he added, "He was impressed, and asked me if I thought you would be interested in a job as writer and assistant editor?"

Maggie's mouth dropped open, but a moment later she said, "Burt, that was my dream the day I left college, but I soon learned that those jobs were reserved for the gals who were willing to spread their legs." She lifted her bar-rag, "And I've been tending bar ever since."

"Yan, asked me," Burt was grinning as he spoke, "If I thought you would be interested in structuring the book as I write it, into chapters that he could begin adding to a serialized section in his magazine." Burt paused when he saw that she was running everything he had just said through her mind.

Maggie was running her fingers back and forth across her lips, with her thumb hooked beneath her jaw. It reminded him of Maverick, his favorite rerun serial, when he was trying to decide whether or not to raise the bet his opponent had made.

Burt finally spoke. "Maggie, Yan said he thought you could probably keep your job, until you decide whether or not to come to Miami and work on the magazine, and structure the stuff I write, before going to work." He grinned, and her stomach still did a flip. "I make very few errors, but I am always so involved in whatever I'm writing, that it must always be restructured." He then chuckled, "Yan had to do it, so I know he's thrilled to have someone who might be able to take that load off his shoulders. He has two new columnists working part time while finishing their time at Miami Uni, so if you decide to marry me and the magazine, you'll have a full time job just editing our work." He grinned wide as he saw her expression change.

"Burt," he could see the devilish mischief in her eyes, "have you ever proposed marriage to another woman?"

"Uh, no...mmm, never even thought about proposing to any of the girls I dated."

The look on his face and his stumbling words, cause Maggie to laugh so hard that tears came, and she had to bend down to catch her breath. Finally she straightened up and started to say something, but began laughing again. Straightening back up, she said after another chuckle, "I thought not."

~ O ~

**B**urt was sitting on the screened in porch of his rented bungalow, looking at the barrier islands a few hundred yards away. The sun was about to drop into the sea. His can of beer was empty, but he loved to watch the sun slowly sink below the horizon.

Scanning the islands that stretched in both directions farther than human eyes could see, he thought about the earliest settlers of Florida, the Calusa Indians. *My god they must have been tough. Even inside this screened porch, those no-see-ums, or as Ab calls 'em, saber-tooth-gnats, would drive me back inside if I didn't have this Avon Skin-So-Soft to rub on every bit of exposed skin. They musta had som'n they put on to keep from goin crazy. Wonder what the hell it was?*

His concentration was broken when a huge osprey swooped down, a short ways beyond the seawall that his temporary home overlooked, and sunk his talons into a big fish and headed back toward the nest to feed her chicks. *That fish was five pounds if it was an ounce. Wonder what kind it was? Damn, wish I could fly like that.*

His concentration was broken again, as the cell phone rang and began its dance across the glass top that his empty beer can was on.

Rick Magers

He saw it was from Yan Shen. "Hello, boss, what's up?" Burt listened closely, because Yan seldom called.

"I just heard about something, Engelbert, that must have been kept under wraps by the Park people and the Chamber of Commerce. The owner of a couple of tour busses in Naples that regularly brings groups to that one hundred year old trading post on Chokoloskee you told me about, has disappeared. He was on a solo kayak trip that was suppose to end at Flamingo in Everglades National Park. He was gonna call an Indian friend, he's from India himself, to pick him up. That was a while back, and he never called, so his friend called Flamingo. I have a friend that has worked there for years, and he calls me now and then when som'n happens that might fit in my magazine, and I cover his weekend barby and beer bill."

When Yan paused, Burt asked, "Where was he last seen?"

"Right there in Chokoloskee. A Ranger put the glasses on a lone guy in a kayak, and he recognised him. He's been bringing groups there for about twenty years. This Ranger, who is also on my tip-list, said he must have put up a tent on one of the islands, and was just getting off that morning to head east toward Flamingo. Hold on, Burt, I have the date he was last seen and his name."

Burt could hear Yan shuffling through his papers as he waited. "It's hear som'rs, Burt, hang on. By the way, he bought a home in a resort half way to Naples, called Port of the Islands. Goddammit, I just had 'em in my hand, sometime yesterday. Anyway, that place he lives in is pretty high-end, and only money people live there, so who knows what mighta happened to him. That place was called Remuda Ranch back in the seventies and eighties. Rumor is that it was once a drop off place for drugs, and at one time the CIA owned the place. Okay, here the sonuvabitch is, lemme see, uh, his name is, or I probably oughta say was, Skilleen Moshhanii, and the Park Ranger saw him on September second when he was paddling east out of Chokoloskee Bay."

"I have several events that happened around here in the manuscript, but haven't bother telling you. I think Maggie's gonna take you up on that offer, so if she does, you'll be reading them soon."

"Okay Eng, I got a call comin in, so check out the tour guide and lemme know. Bye."

Burt closed his phone, and sat there thinking about a guy paddling alone through the Ten Thousand Islands. *I have seen things out there this past few weeks that I would not have thought possible except in some far away primitive land. I hope you're just enjoying yourself too much to bring the trip to a close, but I doubt that's the case.*

~ O ~

Abner heard the rifle shot, and then a man was screaming. As he closed the small exit door behind him, he heard the unmistakable voice of Leon.

"Leave the pistol where it is, asshole, or I'll thread the next bullet through your ears."

Abner flattened against the side of the Quanset and listened as he pulled the pistol out and checked to be sure the chambers were all full. He had no idea what was going on, but he knew that Leon never over-reacted. He simply took care of whatever came up.

The .44 magnum always hung on the exit door's hook whenever he was inside working on something. A swift motion and it was belted around Abner's slim waist before he opened the door.

"That's right," he heard Leon, on the other side of the Quanset say, "gitcher ass back in the car and get the hell outa here, and in case you're thinking about coming back, I've already transferred your face and car tag to a private Black Ops outfit that will send me everything that has ever been entered about you, any goddamn place on the planet. You're in the big league now, Shrek. Y'better rethink your plan before you come back here."

Abner heard a car start, and then he saw headlights bouncing as whoever it was, turned it around. He eased around the corner and called out to Leon, "Okay to come out now, Rambo."

Leon laughed as he stepped off the platform with his sniper rifle hanging from his shoulder on a leather strap, and Susie walking calmly beside him, "Yeah, he came in alone. Rambo, huh?" He chuckled, "Can you picture a crippled up old bastard like me as Rambo?"

Abner grinned and eased the rifle off the old man's shoulder, and then slung it over his, "Yeah, with ole Susie there beside you, you're damn right I can."

Leon just chuckled softly, "C'mon, let's get that pistol, and then see if there's anything on that asshole come in yet."

~ O ~

Earlier that evening, Amad spoke in their language, "You have seemed a bit upset, Jintan, since you arrived from Barranquilla. Is everything alright?"

Jintan turned toward his brother-in-law, and smiled his signature, silver-macabre smile. "Yes, my brother, I am just silently praying to Allah, and asking for His help as we attempt to deal these evil American infidels a deadly blow that will forever cause them to leave our people alone."

"Good." Amad turned briefly toward Jintan, "I should pray to Allah more often." Turning his attention back to the highway, he added softly, almost as though he was alone in the new 2020 Cadillac, "I am too involved in this project."

The vehicle neared the road that ran down to the property owned by Jerome. It had a small shop that sat alone, adjacent to the

Everglades, several miles from the highway. Jintan's mind was strained as he thought, *and a few too many other things, my brother.*

~ O ~

Morris Fent's kidneys caused him to wake up three hours after his deckie, Hussein, had dumped him onto the King-Size bed. He lay there a moment wondering if he had pissed on the bed again. After feeling around with his hand, he realized he had not, and leaped from the bed.

It was a mistake, because the rum still had control of his body. The two strands of linguini with size five feet attached could not support the other eighty pounds. After denting the sheetrock wall with his nearly bald head, Morris lay on his stomach with his right arm beneath him. He was certain that the arm was broken or seriously injured, so he turned his head far enough to the side for him to say, "Rita." He thought she was in bed beside him, so knowing that she was a sound sleeper; he put as much effort into a yell as possible. "**Rita.**" Still nothing, so he yelled again, "**Rita, my goddamn arm is busted.**"

He lay there thinking, *lazy bitch is lyin there laughin' her ass off.* "**Hey, you four quarter whore, I need help.**" Five minutes later, he rolled over on his back. After using his left arm to lift the right, he decided it was not busted so he struggled to his feet.

After feeling his way through the dark, he felt the edge of the bed and turned around to ease his two-hand size ass onto it. "Shit," he groaned when he realized that his kidneys had held out as long as possible.

When they finally emptied, Morris cautiously stood until he was sure his legs would work. Using his hand as a guide sliding along the edge of the now wet mattress, and his feet sliding rather than lifting, he made it to the bedroom door. There was enough moonlight for him to locate the light switch, but when he flipped it—nothing. "Shit." He said and flipped it up and down until he remembered, "The bulb burned out a week or so ago. Shit." *That lazy bitch never has done shit around here.*

His initialed, red Playboy boxer shorts, were soaked, so he shoved them down past his scrawny knees, and then stepped out. He yelled her name a few more times before giving up. *She's probably down the street screwing one of those Honduran boys.* His hand turned the knob of the rear door, *or maybe all of 'em.* He carefully stepped on the first of two steps that led to the floor of the screened porch that had only one screen left on the three sides, and it with a hole big enough to throw a watermelon through, which is exactly what he had done a last July.

He could see his truck sitting near the huge gumbo-limbo tree at the end of the trailer, now that the clouds had passed on by. *Wonder*

Rick Magers

*if that pint of shine is still under the seat?* Morris sat there naked in a lawn chair with only three rubber straps left on the bottom. He slowly stood and shuffled to the doorless doorway, and carefully went down the four steps, which were made of un-mortared concrete blocks.

Halfway to the truck he stumbled on something and fell. *Sonuvabitch, who left that length of septic PVC there? I'd bet a box of crab claws that it was........Oh God!*

The fifteen-foot length of black PVC septic drainpipe had suddenly come alive. It was now over twice that long, and had already sunk its pointed teeth into his neck, and then flipped one coil around Morris' small body.

His short burst of blood curdling screams were heard by his neighbor, whose trailer was on the other side of the gumbo-limbo tree. She was sitting on her screened in porch, which also had few screens left in it. She was once again out on the porch in the wee hours hoping that her husband, Harold, would come home soon.

She turned toward Morris' trailer when she heard the first scream. *He n' Rita are at it again.* She reached down and brought up the pint of MD-20/20 and twisted off the cap, looked at it a moment, and then tossed it into the weeds with a couple hundred other caps. "Mmmmmmmm," she crooned, "ain't nothin quite like Mad Dog to settle a woman's nerves down."

One more scream was heard between loops number two and a

Rick Magers

third — then nothing but the silence of abrupt death.

*Boy oh boy,* his neighbor thought, *them two is sure enough gittin' it on tonight. Well, at least I know she ain't the one with my Harold again.*

Before daylight had lit up the area, the huge python had already completely swallowed Morris, and with a large lump in the middle, had moved back through the busted lattice that went around the bottom of Morris' trailer.

It would begin digesting Morris' small carcass as Hussein and Rita bounced around in the King Size bed above during the next few days.

A few nights later, after Hussein docked Morris's boat, following a good day of pulling crab traps, he was looking down at Rita's naked body. "Now that," nodding at her, "shows what a dumbass Morris was; leaving that for whatever the hell he decided to chase."

"He'll be back. Ain't the first time he jumped in some goddamn floozies' car n' took off, but this time I am not takin him back. I paid for the boat and traps with money I inherited, so you 'n me can look for a place to rent in EC or Chokoloskee, or Hell's Belles, maybe we can find a place on Plantation to buy."

"If we," Hussein said as he shed his clothes, "get on as well out of bed as we do in bed," his grin melted her, "who knows, we just

Rick Magers

might make a damn good team."

Several days later, three young boys were playing in the road that ran right beside Morris and Rita's trailer. She was sleeping late, and Hussein had left with his new deckie at three o'clock in the morning to pull traps that he had moved half way to Marathon in search of crabs.

Rita heard the kids screaming, but ignored them and rolled over and went back to sleep. She was awakened a short time later when she heard sirens wailing next to her bedroom window. She dressed and went outside.

The old woman next door told her that the kids had seen a bunch of snakes coming out from beneath Rita's trailer, and ran to her trailer and told her about them.

"I juss figgered," she said, "that they had seen some big night crawlers like I use to catch shell crackers. When I got there, though, here was about twenty little snakes a'wanderin in and out, under your trailer. I opened my new smart-phone and called the Poleece. Hey," the old woman excitedly yelled and pointed, "they's got another one o' them dang snakes."

Rita watched as the Animal Rescue officers collected the baby snakes and tossed them into burlap bags. The Sherriff's Deputy had called them as soon as she arrived and saw the baby pythons going in and out of the busted lattice bordering the old trailer.

Rick Magers

Before nightfall, one hundred and three baby pythons had been caught and bagged by a force of thirty Animal Rescue officers. A team of experienced python handlers had located the mother under Rita's trailer, and put cable snares around her neck. After hooking her body to three, fifty-pound weights to inhibit her ability to loop around anyone, or anything, they pulled the python out from under the trailer and then euthanized her.

She measured twenty-three feet exactly, and later, at the Animal Rescue compound in Naples she was opened up. Human bones were found, and a titanium knee that was traced by serial number to Morris Fent. A gold pocket watch with his name on it was also found inside the snake.

When Rita was later informed, she said, "Good, now I don't hafta worry about that worthless sonuvabitch comin home."

~ O ~

**P**ercy was halfway back to Tallahassee when his cell phone rang.

He looked at the screen to see who was calling and almost threw the phone out the window.

Instead, he shoved it back into the holder on his dash and pressed the button on his earpiece. "Just return from Moscow, Trotsky?"

"Moscow," the Russian said in very broken English, "what the fuck would I be doing in Moscow?"

"Damned if I know, but I been waiting a week for you to give me some goddamn information on that swamp guy. I figured you got homesick and went home for some TLC."

"I was locked up, and didn't wanna call you on their pay phone, because they're always bugged."

"Seems t'me that you coulda kept your ass outa jail long enough t'get me some background on that guy."

"Got it right here in front of me, boss." He was too wired up to pause, so he continued, "The guy's an ex-Army Ranger or Green Beret or som'n like that, and his dead daddy's pal lives out there in a shack or som'n. He was an Army sniper for about thirty years, or maybe twenty, but he retired and worked for the fukin CIA as their snoop and sniper, whatever, but he finally retired to work with his dead drug smuggler pal's kid, and…"

"Yeah, yeah, Trotsky, I already learned that the hard way. Got half a goddamn thumb now, all because the fukker that I didn't know was out there shot my pistol outa my hand." Percy refused to let the Russian get a word in, "I'm halfway back to Tallahassee now to try to get my thumb sewed up, and my shit together again. Hey, about that grand I was gonna give ya. Well, I'm gonna give it, and probably a few more, to a surgeon to get m'thumb workin again."

He pressed the off button on his earpiece, and it switched the phone off.

*Goddamn if I ain't got a gift for finding the sorriest buncha fukkers on this bloody planet to work with. Gotta git off this damn I-75 and find a Cracker Barrel.*

~ O ~

Livingston Maule and Senator Pierpont were having a casual lunch at the Golden Albatross Country Club that catered only to Tallahassee's wealthy and powerful members.

The senator said softly while leaning forward, "You heard from Percy, lately?"

Without looking away from the area around the pool outside that was teeming with the young thong-wearing beauties that filled the place each summer, the short round man said, "Yeah he'll be hear any minute."

The two men had just ordered their second drink, and a busboy was clearing the table of food ware, when Percy walked in.

"G'day mates," Percy said with a chortle and his version of carefree charisma, which was more often than not, considered an attitude of 'I'm big, mean, and do not give a shit.'

"Care for a drink, Percy?" Senator Pierpont asked.

"I 'ave never turned down a bloody free drink in me life, mate, thanks."

While the Senator motioned for the cocktail waitress to come take Percy's order, Livingston Maule sipped his Brandy Alexander and looked at Percy.

Aware he was being scrutinized by the fat billionaire, Percy chatted with the Senator. When his bottle of Red Stripe arrived, he took a sip from the bottle and turned toward the land developer, "Bloody good beer, mate, I'd 'afta say it's close to Cascade, me favorite that's made at the brewery on Tasmania." He held the bottle up to the huge window overlooking the thong bunnies at the pool to look over the contents. "Beautiful color, eh?" He held it so Livingston could see it.

"Looks like beer."

"Ha," Percy laughed softly, "beer is like women; seem to be all the same until you've 'ad a taste of a spectacularly great one." He sipped from the bottle before sitting it back down, then turned to Livingston, "Well mate, what is it you wanted to talk about?"

Without hesitation, Livingston said, "What are you planning to do about the situation down in that swamp city?"

"Well mate, if I 'ad a buncha Navy SEAL Team blokes as me pals, or mebbe a dozen'r so Army Rangers t'go on our payroll, we'd go back down and bury that group of guys I told you about. But since I don't, I reckon we'll be forced t'find another way around the bloody problem." He looked straight at Livingston, "Whadaya think ought t'be done now, mate?"

Livingston paused for a full minute, and looked hard at Percy. Finally, after a sip of his cocktail, he spoke so softly that Percy was forced to lean toward the man to hear him. "What I think should be done first, before we consider an alternative approach to this problem down south, is that we'll settle the problem that we have right here."

Percy sipped his beer and stalled as he considered the situation. "Bloody great beer, this stuff, 'ave you been to Jamaica, Livingston?"

The billionaire's diamond-hard, unblinking eyes were still focused on Percy. "Twenty years ago I bought fifty acres just inland of Negril, and have an estate there to go to during the winter." Livingston sat back and slowly unwrapped a new, hand-rolled cigar that he ordered by the case from Havana.

Finally, Percy spoke in a softer, almost humble tone of voice, "What bloody problem do we 'ave right 'ere, mate?"

"You left here a short while back," Livingston said, "with two hundred thousand dollars of my money. You were not able to fulfill your contract, so, considering twenty-five thousand for expenses, you are still holding quite a large amount on my money," he now leaned forward to prevent anyone but the three of them from hearing, "that I want back before the sun sets tomorrow."

Percy covered the fact that he was frightened, but he was. He had always thoroughly researched anyone that he planned to do business with, but he had rushed into this situation in Everglades City, and did not take time to do it. Once he put a fresh gauze wrapping on his thumb, he sat at his computer and entered Maule Industries into the private detective agency that he had been using since he settled in Tallahassee. He kept $5,000 on their books, so they would begin work immediately when he contacted them.

Percy checked a small square that had Full Disclosure beside it, and even knowing it would cost him a bundle, he wished he had done it earlier. He hit the Enter key and leaned back to sip the last of the cognac in the small glass.

Percy had gone downstairs to be certain that every-thing in his club was on track, and then had the Chef prepare him two lobster tails, a stuffed baked potato, and a bowl of shrimp bisque. All to be sent upstairs on the dumb-waiter to his apartment.

Two hours later the dirty dishes had been sent back down, and he sat sipping Martell Creation Cognac again. It was a gift from the Florida Governor and arrived by private messenger in a hand carved Baccarat Decanter. It was a $7,500 gift for sending a senator to St. Lucia for a week with his number one on-call girl, Lilly.

When the email finally came, Percy read it twice. He had known from the first that Livingston Maule was not a run-of-the-mill stuffed, fat little toad. However, he had never considered the billionaire to be a dangerous man to be doing business with. He now knew better. *Damn*, Percy thought, *that fuck-happy fat little shit has been imbedded with the goddamn mob since he was a kid growing up in the Bronx.*

He got another chilled glass from the built-in fridge in his gigantic hardwood desk, and poured it full. Leaning back, he sipped as his mind raced. *Might be a good time to return to Oz for a while to let this shit blow over.*

Half way to the bottom of the small crystal glass, he had made up his mind. After ordering a one-way ticket to Sydney, he called downstairs and explained to his new club manager that his dear mother was sick, and he was leaving in the morning for Australia. "Please arrange for a taxicab to pick me up downstairs at exactly six AM in the morning."

After Percy hung up the phone, his manager glanced around to be certain nobody was near enough to hear. He then dialed the phone.

~ O ~

As Amad drove the Cadillac north along the highway toward the gravel road, Jintan's mind replayed a conversation that took place in Barranquilla. Amad's superior, Ali Mohammad Nabavvi, had sent a messenger to meet him at the hanger where the Mallard was being thoroughly checked out before departure. The man gave Jintan the operation code in Iranian, and handed Jintan a cell phone. "Ali Mohammad Nabavvi," the man said, "is waiting now for your call. I will wait until you have spoken with him."

Jintan nodded, and then walked to the rear of the hanger to get away from the noise of arriving and departing airliners. The phone rang twice and was answered, "Jintan, Ali Mohammad Nabavvi said, I want you to listen very carefully, because you may soon have it in your power to save our revolution against those infidels. I love Amad as though he is my birth brother, but he has become a new man these past two years. Do you know of his concubine in Miami?"

"No sir, I do not."

"She is a blond young American, whose beauty blinded Amad when he met her two years ago." He paused to allow Jintan's mind to grasp what he had just told him. "She has her own condo on Miami Beach that he gifted her with, and drives a new Porsche every six months." Another pause caused Jintan's eyes to narrow, but nothing else showed. "Her personal bank account," Ali Mohammad Nabavvi, continued, "has already reached one million American dollars. If this current operation in the Florida swamp goes well, then you will replace Amad, and I will bring him to me for counsel. But, if the Americans have learned of our plans, and intercept you at any point along the way, I must trust you, as the most devout of our people, to join Amad as martyrs." Ali Mohammad Nabavvi paused to let what he said flow through

Jintan's mind. After half a minute, he spoke again. "I have known you since you were born, Jintan, and consider you to be the most trusted among our people, which is why I am trusting you with this information. If Amad is captured alive, the information that he has acquired would, I fear, be readily given to his torturers. The young man that brought you the phone is my grandson, and is a devout believer in our mission to forever rid our nation of the American infidels.

~ O ~

Maggie was behind the bar at the Seafood Junction when she noticed a small young woman holding the hand of a very cute little girl. They had entered through a screen door that takes you directly into the chickee bar, rather than in through the restaurant's main door.

Maggie said, "Hi, betcha came through the wrong door, dincha?" Her smile was so friendly and open, that the young woman came to her grinning.

"I am still learning English, so you maybe will have to help me with words." Her small, doll-like brown face opened into a wide smile. "I think I was taking my daughter inside the restaurant to meet my boyfriend."

"That's okay, darlin', lots of people do the same thing. Maggie grinned, "And some of 'em never make it on into the dining room."

"Oh, good, then I am not the only dummy." Her giggle was so child-like that Maggie began giggling, and then the little girl did too.

While Maggie was giggling, she was making a drink. She leaned against the bar and offered it to the little girl, "This is a Shirley Temple, and it's kinda like a no alcohol cocktail for kids."

She looked at her mother, who said, "You can have it, Angelina. I drank one when Angelo brought me here one day for lunch." She grinned up at Maggie, and then down at her daughter, "And he drank one too." Her childish giggle made Maggie feel like coming around and hugging her.

"I bet," Maggie said looking down at the child that was sipping the sweet drink and smiling, "that you are Angelina, and this," she nodded at the young woman, "is your mommy, Christina." She grinned when she saw the look on the woman's face, "No magic or anything like that involved. My boyfriend is a writer and heard about Angelina's ordeal with the python, and told me about it. I was pretty sure it was you that I've seen several times in Everglades City."

"You see me in town?" the woman asked, and then the little girl said in perfect English, "you see me before, too?"

"Yep, at the market a couple of times, and at the Post Office mailing a package one day. I was pretty sure it was you, because my boyfriend said it was a very pretty young woman and an adorable little girl that his friend pointed out. He's writing a book about this area and is hoping to visit with you both to learn all about the day the python tried to steal Angelina."

She turned to see a man and woman climbing up on stools. "I have customers, so please sit down until I come back, and I'll fix you both a Shirley Temple." Before the woman could speak, Angelina was climbing up onto the stool saying, "Yep, okay, me an mommy will be here."

~ O ~

"Gentlemen, first I wanna thank y'all for coming here to this meeting. Many of you know me, but for the sake of those who don't, my name is Abner Brown. Except for my time spent in the Army, I have lived in Everglades City and the surrounding swamp, all my life. I don't like long-winded meetings, so I'm gonna make this one short and to the point.

Governor Skip Halsey has appointed me to lead this group of professional hunter/trappers. We've all been running airboats through the Everglades for many years, and understand how it works. When airboat permits to allow us to hunt pythons were first offered, too many men who received them were not qualified.

I helped trim the permit holders down to the twelve people, including myself, that are now in this room. Each permit is limited to one of the twelve sections shown on the map that I am now pulling down." Abner's hand was on the bottom handle attached to a large map inside a roll-down tube, fastened to the wall behind him.

Once the map was down, and the handle put over a hook in the wooden wall, he stepped back. Waving his hand in an arc at the map, he said, "There are the twelve areas, and one is assigned to each of us. Mine if number one, which you can see is considerable smaller that the rest. We did that because I will be assisting y'all regularly to be certain that we're getting as many pythons as is humanly possible." He paused a moment to let them absorb what they had heard.

"The state is providing each of us with a GPS that is loaded with this map. We'll all know where we are at all times, and where we located pythons. I have them with me and will give each of you one before you leave. Boys, when I first went after those snakes back in two thousand and eight, I felt very confident that me and a few guys here today, could eventually get 'em all." He chuckled, "Boy, was I wrong."

Abner smiled as he heard a deep voice say, "Oh yeah buddy, we sure was."

"We now know," he continued, "that the pythons will be like

Rick Magers

the hyacinth that was introduced to Florida in the eighteen eighties. We will never get rid of them, but they can be brought under control if all twelve of us work together."

Abner began digging through an old leather briefcase that once belonged to his father. "Ah, here it is." He held up a folded sheet of yellow lined paper. "Made m'self some notes while I was in Tallahassee. Y'all are gonna like this. Governor Halsey personally pushed this bill through, and had it entered into the state's record. We will now legally, only be required to bring in the python's head. We've been doin it for a while, but never knew if it would be changed, and we'd hafta bring in the entire damn snake in again." Abner sipped a cup of coffee he's brought with him. Eeeyuk!" He shoved the cup away. "Guess I'm gettin too damned long winded after all—stuff's cold."

He grinned when he heard the same deep voice, "You Juss take yer time, Ab, this here's the part I'm most intrested in."

"The Florida Governor contacted the state's zoologist," Abner continued, "and told her to determine how to make a guage that'll tell how long a python is just by the head. I reckon it'll be like the crawfish or stone crab guages. It'll probably be the distance between the eyes, or mebbe the distance from the nose to the eyes, or som'n like that. Main thing though, is that we'll get paid for the head as if it was the entire snake, and we won't be arguing about how long the sucker was."

Rick Magers

Abner ruffled through his briefcase again and come out with another sheet torn off a yellow tablet. "Okay, I found it. We'll get a hundred dollars a foot for fifteen footers and up, and then seventy-five a foot for the seven to fifteen footers, and fifty for all under seven.

The govenor's secretary will call me as soon as Doctor Louise Chen, the zoologist, has the guage figured out. In the meantime, measure your python, and then take a picture of it with a yardstick that is lying on it from the tip of its nose back. Jim sells them at the hardware if you don't have one.

One more bit of information I'm gonna give y'all before we leave. My number is on a card that I placed in each GPS box. There's money t'be made sellin the skins and meat, and if you can find a place to sell it, then go for it. If you can't, then call me and I'll tell you what I pay for meat and skins. I really have about all I can do to just keep up with my own damn snakes, but if you can't find a place to sell yours, then call me n' I'll give you as good a price as I can." He looked at his watch, "That didn't take too long, so c'mon over here n' gitcher GPS and let's all get back to the swamp n' make some money."

~ O ~

Samson Blackraven had asked one of his men to bring him a black cup of coffee. He was sipping it when the beeper on his video console went off. He hit the blue button on the NORAD panel and immediately General Masterson was there in front of him. "Update, Samson, the water bird has just now left the Keys and is heading straight for a meeting with our Navy SEAL teams. Over and standing by."

Samson always tried to cover all possibilities of bad communications between operatives, so he pressed the button that always connected him to the officer in charge of the ground forces, wherever the hell they were. "Hello, Captain MacGregor, Blackraven here, did you get the latest Intel on Big Bird?"

"Yessir, the General just a moment ago to inform me that she'll soon be here. We're ready for her."

"Good, just checking to be sure. Please let me know when the baggage is secured. Over and standing by."

~ O ~

As the Cadillac rolled smoothly along the highway, Jintan's mind had replayed the last of Ali Mohammad Nabavvi's message for the fifth time since the phone call in Barranquilla. *I trust Jintan, that you will allow my grandson to fit you into the explosive vest he has with him, and show you how to use the detonator. And, if my worst fears are met by*

Rick Magers

*you and Amad, you will use it. Allah will be with you, my brother."*
Jintan closed his eyes tight and said another prayer to Allah. He
opened them wide when he felt the smooth ride change.

Amad had just turned the black Cadillac east onto the gravel
road that ran to Jerome's property, where the five terrorists were to
dock the five airboats. Halfway along the road, they spotted the
two Hummers that he had purchased months earlier. Each was
parked off the side of the road, one on each side, facing them with
their lights off. Five specially trained Jihadists were in each vehicle,
and were armed with AK-47 automatic rifles. Their orders were to
stop any vehicle that approached, and if it was not Amad and
Jintan, they were to execute everyone inside and have a man drive
the vehicle to Jerome's shop and hide it.

Jintan had known of Amad's mistress for several months. Odd
scents and mannerisms had caused him to wonder. His devotion to
his country's Jihad wars against all who encroach on the way-of-life
in Iran caused him to follow his mentor and brother-in-law, Amad.

When Jintan learned of Amad's young mistress, he had begun
regularly praying to Allah, rather than speak to Amad about it. He
asked Allah to help Amad see the errors of his actions, and return
to his wife in Iran, Jintan's sister.

The minute that Amad turned the Cadillac onto the gravel road,
Jintan had casually reached into his pocket. Fumbling in the
darkness, he made certain that the small detonating device was

positioned correctly in his hand. Never once did he consider not following his holy leader, Ali Mohammad Nabavvi's instructions.

Amad pulled the Cadillac ahead as he activated his window. Expecting to see the man that he had placed in charge of this ten-man defense team, he was shocked to see several masked Navy SEALS. By the time his brain focused on the predicament he was in, Amad was on his way to martyrdom in the company of his devoted brother-in-law. Whether or not they would be met by a bevy of sexy young nubile concubines, to make their eternal stay way up in paradise pleasurable, will never be known by mortals.

What instantly became fact though, was that the two terrorists inside were vaporized by the blast, and that their vehicle was destroyed. Thanks to new technology, only two men in Navy SEAL teams were slightly injured. Their knowledge of the dangers of roadside roadblocks was hard-won during the years they were deployed in hostile areas such as Afghanistan.

They were all wearing the very latest anti-blast gear, and had been trained to never approach a vehicle too close. Their schooling dictated that they demand the occupants to get out of the vehicle and lay prone on the ground facedown with their hands opened palm-up.

During subsequent interviews by their superiors, they all entered one request. "Please tell our boys in the think-tanks to work on something that will protect our ears. We're all still hearing the Bells of Saint Mary."

~ O ~

Captain MacGregor and four of his SEAL team 8 men were all in position in airboats at the landing site. They were two miles from Jerome's property where the terrorists were to take the packages they would have on the airboats. Each SEAL was unshaven and dressed as a common waterman. The weapon they would use to kill the five terrorists was their trusted Heckler & Koch laser-aiming Mk 23 Mod O semi-automatic pistol with suppressor, firing the trusted man-stopping .45 ACP.

Each member of SEAL team 7 was in his own small well camouflaged rubber boat that was anchored fore and aft to stabilize it. Several mock test-landings by experienced Mallard pilots had narrowed the landing spot down. If things did not go as planned, they could sever both anchor ropes, start the tiny ten-horse-power engine, and be at the scene of action within seconds.

Captain MacGregor's two best men with the hand-held, retractable buttstock, FN MK Grenade Launcher, were positioned in their camouflaged rubber boats to ensure that if all of their plans went awry, the Mallard would be destroyed.

~ O ~

Less than twenty minutes after Amad and Jintan had unexpec-

tedly caught the skybus to the terrorist version of Valhalla, the Mallard pilots had the two flashing buoys in site, and were aiming their water bird at the touchdown spot to be right in the middle between the two beacons.

"Fire 'em up boys," Captain MacGregor said into the wireless mic sewn into the front of the collar of the old windbreaker he was wearing, "she's comin in."

The airboat engines all started instantly. Their pistol with noise suppressor was in a leather holster on the side of the frame that held the seat where the operator sat looking down. A dark rag had been draped over the holster in case one of the terrorists happened to look that way.

While each of the five airboats ran slowly along, as the flying boat, not far away, came to a stop. SEAL team 7 had seen the Mallard touch down on the water exactly where they all hoped it would. They pulled their anchors up and placed them in the rubber boat. Each man sat silent and motionless in the tiny camouflaged rubber boat, one hundred yards away. They monitored the action through the night-vision device attached to their helmet.

Captain MacGregor's airboat was the last to jockey up to the door of the Mallard. His terrorist placed the last two boxes into the airboat, stepped in, and then waved at the copilot to close the door. Ten seconds later, as the engines on the Mallard roared and began pulling the bird through the water, Captain MacGregor said softly into his mic, "Now, on three."

If it could have somehow been filmed, the actions of the five Navy Seals would appear to have been the result of many long hours working with a professional Holly-wood choreographer.

As had previously been decided, each SEAL turned his airboat towards the land base where they had waited for the arrival of the Mallard, and throttled ahead just enough to cause the terrorists to bend down and grab the gunwale for support.

Five shots were followed by five more—all headshots. Five more terrorists were now following the ten Jihadists from the two Hummers that were supposed to prevent anyone from entering. Amad and Jintan were going to have plenty of company in Valhalla.

Two minutes after the shots were fired, three Marine helicopters flew in and lit up the entire area. Had either the pilot of the Mallard or his copilot looked back, they would have seen the lights, but they were both busy, and were concentrating on remaining below 100 feet altitude until they crossed over the Florida Keys, and flew on to the area near the submarine base on Andros Island. There they would climb up to altitude for the trip home to Barranquilla, as if they had just taken off from the AUTEC airstrip.

~ O ~

Maggie was tending to a busy bar on a clear sunny Saturday afternoon, when she heard a crowd outside in the parking lot laughing. She was too busy to investigate, so she kept pouring drinks and drawing draft beers.

As the owner, Billy Potter, came through the doors out to the Chickee Bar, all of her customers climbed down from their stools simultaneously and headed outside.

Billy looked toward Maggie with a scowling face. "I want you to see how much you've cost me, Maggie." He motioned with his arm, "Just look at the empty barstools and imagine how much money I just lost. C'mon, follow me outside and see for yourself." He went to the screen door and held it open until a very confused Maggie came out from behind the bar and headed toward him.

Everyone from her chickee bar, and all of the diners from inside The Seafood Junction, plus everyone that had worked there, were outside looking up toward the sky.

Maggie followed their gaze, and then when she finally saw it, she laughed so hard that she was forced to bend over to catch her breath. Everyone began laughing, and when she saw Billy, he was grinning from ear to ear.

She looked up as the two airplanes flew by again, one a little higher than the other and behind a bit. She smiled as she silently read, *Will you please marry me, Maggie.* Her smile widened when she read the sign the second plane was towing. *Please, please, Maggie, I love you.*

As the two planes made their last pass before heading back to the Naples Airport, Burt walked up behind her and kneeled down saying loudly, "Maggie will you marry me and accept this ring and my never ending love?"

She spun around so fast that she almost fell, but some of the people who had crowded around them held her up. Tears were flowing down her beautiful Irish face and her red hair seemed to be on fire and dancing in the thin breeze.

"Well," Burt said as he grinned up at her.

"Well, lemme think about it." Maggie said with a rigid frown.

Burt's mouth dropped open, but slammed shut when Maggie started laughing, and then said, "Yes, absolutely yes." She smiled and wiped away the tears as he stood and pulled the diamond engagement ring from the case and slipped it on her finger.

Rick Magers

The laughing crowd cheered when they heard Billy's voice in the hand-held battery operated megaphone, "Free drinks for everyone until five, and I'm tending bar. Maggie is off early with full pay."

Burt held Maggie as he said, "See how fast a loving crowd abandons you when free drinks are offered." They both laughed and went inside to mingle with all the people that were in on it.

As soon as they were inside, Maggie pointed, "Look who is sitting over there, Burt."

"That's the little girl the python almost got. Let's go say hello."

Before they were even to the table, Angelina's smile was quickly spreading across her adorable brown face. "Shirley Temple lady," she said, and waved.

"Hello Christina, hello Angelina and this must be," she nodded at the young man sitting between them, "Angelo, your fiancé."

"Yes, Maggie," Christina smiled and nodded at Burt, "and that must be the man who hired Angelo's uncles to fly the proposal signs."

"Yes, his name is Burt."

"Hello Burt," Christina said, followed by a very shy Angelo saying the same thing with a big smile. Angelina just smiled up at him.

"I hope," Burt said, "that I can come by your home on a day that both of you are home, so I can hear the story about your daughter

Rick Magers

being attacked by a large python. I would love to add it to a book about this area that I'm writing."

"I can tell you the story," Angelina said, and before anyone could speak, she began. "I was walking along a road where my new daddy works on his fish boat." She took a deep breath and continued, "A big snake tried to eat me, but Superman came and killed it with his big fish knife." She smiled wide and folded both hands out beside her tiny shoulders, palms up, adding, "And here I am, still alive to live happily ever after."

One of the servers was Maggie's friend from their college days in Miami. She had moved to Everglades City one year earlier. She asked if she could bring them all something to drink.

"Sure Sue," she turned back to Christina, "I really think I know what Angelina wants, but how about you and Angelo?"

"We would like the same that Angelina will drink."

"Okey dokey," Burt said with a smile at the little girl sitting beside him, "we'll have five Shirley Temples."

While all the drinks were being made by Billy Potter, Maggie asked Christina if they had set a date yet for the wedding.

"Oh yes," the obviously thrilled young woman said, "it will be on Angelo's cousin's fishing boat next Friday evening. He is a licensed Captain, just like Angelo, and is going to clean the boat real good and put Christmas lights on it. Just a small group of our friends, and Mister and Missus Grayson, the people who adopted me and Angelina, will ride out the channel with us to watch the ceremony. When we come back, Angelo and I will pack everything we are taking with us on our honeymoon."

"Oh," Maggie said, "that sounds like a wonderful wedding. Where are you going on your honeymoon?"

"All three of us," Christina said while smiling at her daughter, "are going back home for two weeks to our birthplace in Limon Honduras." She turned back to Maggie, "Would you and your husband-to-be, like to ride on the boat to see our wedding?"

"I would love to," she turned to Burt, "how about you?"

"Wouldn't miss it for the world."

## ~ O O ~

Delvin Watson said, "I was in my airboat looking around for a sign of pythons, when I thought I spotted one. After tossing the airboat's anchor into the swamp brush at the edge of the big hammock, I pulled slowly on the rope and eased on in. After an hour on foot, tracking its path, I suddenly began having serious second thoughts. This critter does not move at all like a reticulated python, or any other type of python that I've ever seen.

Another silent ten minutes and I knew that I was getting close because there was a little water remaining in its gracefully swerving path, whatever 'it' was. Tiny mice are still running up n' down my neck.

A moment later, I eased up to a slight mound that the path had only recently gone over. Using the sniper skills that I learned well as a Green Beret, during three tours in Viet Nam. I eased up as my disbelieving eyes saw something that my mind refused to accept.

Easing slowly back until I knew there was now room under the thick canopy of extended tree limbs, and brush that had used them as growing platforms; I bolted up and ran for my life, literally."

## ~ O O ~

Only six short miles northwest of where Delvin had seen something frightening enough to cause a decorated member of the elite Green Beret to turn around and run, Charlie Booker was inside a slightly smaller but considerably more dense hammock.

Charlie was born in Immokalee but had grown up in Ochopee, a small town on Tamiami Trail. Ochopee is the home of the popular tourist attraction and Everglades Zoo, Wooten's Airboat Tours. It is a huge attraction only a few miles east of Highway 29.

Rick Magers

Charlie had never spent time in the military, but he had done time—three years in a Federal Pen for getting careless and allowing a young new gung-ho Everglades National Park Ranger to bust him while bringing in three wet bales of Colombian marijuana.

Charlie was quite famous among the local people for his poaching skills. Elwood Brown once said, "Ole Charlie kin sneak up on a Curlew sittin on a nest of eggs an steal 'em out from under her witout thet damn Curlew even knowin he was there." He laughed hard for a moment before adding, "I betcha he's driven a buncha curlew and other birds out there in the swamp, crazy as a loon wondering where'd m'damn eggs go?"

Charlie moved a little farther into the hammock, and then stopped to look and listen. He repeated this tact each few feet he moved ahead. He was looking for an area that he knew was inside this hammock. Charlie was one of the best trackers of the reticulated pythons that in the last few years had stripped the Everglades of much of the indigenous wildlife.

His wealth had grown considerably larger since he had learned how to locate a clutch of python eggs, and by using science that he learned on the Internet, and from working for a short time with Abner Brown. His new knowledge let him accurately determine when, within a forty-eight hour span, they would hatch.

Government leaders refused to listen to the very few knowledgeable men like Charlie, Delvin, and Abner, who had all suggested a larger bounty. They had spoken to the five men in Tallahassee, who were placed in charge of the 'Save Our Everglades' project, and any other Florida politician who would listen. Had these men just listened to them, and had placed a larger bounty on the pythons; there would still today be many of the animals that had been in the Everglades for centuries.

Typically, though, once Charlie left Tallahassee, back in 2015, they laughed like the idiots they really were. The small bounty they finally decided to offer was not enough to pay the fuel bill for the airboat owners, now that it was averaging over $6 per gallon.

A few men brought in some small pythons, and the alien beasts kept right on breeding and multiplying. There are now so many pythons out there, that the only way to get rid of them was to fill in the entire Everglades with soil, which was probably the political goal, all along.

When that happens, the property that was once the Everglades, will be worth more than Dubai, which was also filled in to create a playground for the rich and famous.

The upside of that terrible decision will be: two more international airports, several gated communities where wealthy Snow Birds can live out their days. Disneyglades will be a re-created section with artificial environment and wildlife that will let paying customers see what the only 'River of Grass' on the planet, once looked like. Tram tour customers will regularly be threatened by plastic alligators, crocodiles, thirty-foot-long pythons, and God only knows what other creatures the Disneyglades geniuses will come up with.

The downside of that terrible decision will be: water bills in the Greater Miami area will skyrocket to prices that only the wealthy can pay. $1500 monthly water bills (or perhaps much higher) will chase the common working class from Southeast Florida, like rats from a sinking English ship.

"Why," they will wonder, "is our water bill so high?" Because a wonderful gift that the one-and-only Everglades had, without their knowledge, brought to the residents of the Greater Miami area was inexpensive fresh water. The only 'River of Grass' on the planet, created the aquifer of fresh water that held the salt water down, and kept it out of their sinks, toilets, showers, and swimming pool. In addition, it allowed them to have their chauffeur wash their cars daily.

Now finely, the wealthy segment of the Greater Miami area will see their dreams come true. No more common working people driving their disgusting two or three year old cars and trucks will be seen in New Miami. Busses will bring in the needed workers, and at the end of their work shift, they will be taken back to their hovels beyond the eight-foot-tall walls surrounding the sacred soil of Greater Miami. Fortunes will be spent wiping out the memory of those days when common people walked freely among beautiful

Rick Magers

people of Greater Miami.

The government idiots finally relented, and in 2020 they bumped up the old bounty to $400. Nobody went out. $500 a month later, and still no locals fired up their airboats. Rangers ran back and forth like a fox that had stumbled upon an abandoned nest full of eggs.

The Park Rangers brought in 12 pythons in six months and knocked a small dent in the $312,000 fuel bill for that period.

In 2023 a new department was created: Everglades National Park Service Intelligence Department. It soon became an oxymoron that was the source of a great many cynical jokes among the locals... "Dumb and Dumber just brought in another fifty thousand dollar python."

**B**etter minds prevailed and the python bounty soon went up. Abner, Charlie, Delvin, and the others began making a serious dent in the amount of pythons living in the Everglades.

~ O O ~

**O**ne last look around, and then he listened for noise that did not belong there. Charlie slowly lifted his head up above the mound he had just come to. His eyes were not ready for what he saw. Two emotionless cold eyes like no other eyes he had ever seen were locked onto his. A panic he had never before felt caused him to abandon all caution.

Charlie abruptly stood and prepared to run, but the fifteen-foot long snake's huge open mouth had locked onto his arm.

Charlie was able to scream only two words before his world abruptly went black— "**It's not**…………

~ O O ~

**I**n July 2014, a young man and his wife had rented a small cottage on the outskirts of Atlanta, Georgia. He had recently secured a job at Stone Mountain Park, and they were thrilled to be settling in the booming Georgia city.

Lars Jannsen slipped quietly from the bed and stood looking down on his sleeping wife. He smiled as she moved her lips; grimacing slightly as last night's wine wiped all traces of moisture from her mouth. *Probably shouldn't have opened that last bottle, but I wanted her to sleep late this morning.*

In the bathroom, Lars stood a moment in front of the full-length mirror on the door and inspected his naked five-foot-nine-inch, perfectly sculptured body. *Gerta,* he smiled at his unabashed cockiness, *you were one lucky little Kraut to get me.* Grinning, he then stepped quietly into the shower. He did not want to risk waking her, so he kept the water on low and just sponged off.

Gerta had fallen asleep soon after their private little two-person-party the previous night. Lars carried all of the clothes he would wear today into the living room of the tiny cottage they had rented six months earlier—after returning from their honeymoon.

"It's certainly a nice location," Gerta had commented after looking through the rundown little shack, "but it's gonna need a lotta fixing up, darling. That window in the laundry room will go up, but it won't close all the way."

"Don't worry babe," Lars had assured her, "I'll have this place in shape in no time."

A week later the front door still did not have a security latch, and the little laundry room window still would not close all the way.

### ~ Fatal procrastination ~

Lars pushed in the button on the front door then gently closed it

Rick Magers

behind him. He heard the click then tested to be sure it was securely locked before heading toward his car in the early morning darkness. The stifling Georgia heat was already making him sweat as he entered the five-year-old Porsche. Moments later he sighed, "Ahhhh, air-conditioning," and then turned the corner and began the one hour drive to Stone Mountain where he worked.

Two cold, calculating, emotionless, cruel eyes watched Lars leave the little house. They had been watching for an hour—he could exercise patience as few can when they are hunting. His soft movements were slow and silent as he moved forward toward the partially open window; a predator seldom equaled. He very carefully studies all of his victims and is never in a hurry—NEVER! He has killed many, many times without being caught.

He stopped several times while closing the gap. All senses so finely tuned to his quest that he could see a small cockroach walking along the windowsill several feet ahead. Two field mice paused at the window before entering—they did not go un-noticed. He turned in every direction, carefully looking for any signs of movement before continuing to the window.

His entry was as silent as the ghosts that travel through a frightened person's mind. Once inside the room he remained motionless for ten minutes as he allowed the entire contents of the little house to be absorbed into his brain. It was a brain that could hear a sound others could not, and analyze it for potential danger—the ultimate predator that cares not when or where he locates his next victim.

Once satisfied that he was in safe territory, he moved through the flimsy drapes covering the laundry room doorway. Halfway to the opening ahead he heard a noise that froze him in his tracks.

Wine did two things to Gerta. Made her feel good and made her pee. The feel good of last evening's hours with Lars was gone. *Gotta pee now*, she thought as she climbed from the bed.

After her inflated kidneys had emptied into the bowl, she wiped herself and looked at her naked body in the same mirror that her husband often used. *Yech! Yer a mess, girl.*

All of the killer's senses were now on full alert, as he listened to the movement on the other side of the door. He had not yet put his hood on before he entered, because he had not thought it necessary. It was now in place though, as he checked to be certain that his weapons to kill with, were ready. He advanced slowly as his eyes searched the area ahead, while moving across the floor. He was now armed and ready for action. The room was empty.

A shadow moved in the light coming from beneath the closed door ahead, and he moved silently but swiftly to the door and waited. The thrill of a new killing surged through his system like a deadly tsunami finally reaching the shore.

After a few more drops left her kidneys, Gerta wiped herself again, and then stood looking at her naked body as the toilet flushed. She fluffed her hair then placed both hands on her slender hips. As her eyes roamed the entire length of her one-hundred-pound, five-foot-tall frame, she said aloud, "Not too bad."

When the young woman opened the bathroom door to go back to bed for a while, the silently stalking, deadly intruder, struck with such precision that she was already dying as she slumped to the cracked-linoleum covered floor. A moment before he struck, Gerta had looked into the cold eyes in the center of the hooded intruder's face and felt terrifying horror of intensity far greater than most are ever unfortunate enough to experience.

Not as the result of compassion, because there was none, but due to his ability to kill swiftly, Gerta was spared a lingering death. She was no longer alive as he moved back into the outside nighttime shadows, from which he had silently and covertly come.

Before dawn, the silent killer slipped into a truckload of needed merchandise on its way from Atlanta to Miami. Once securely

Rick Magers

snuggled beneath the front of the load he closed his eyes and slept. At a nighttime coffee stop outside of Miami, he silently slipped from the truck and went into the tall grass that led to the adjacent Everglades. For the first time in a long time, he felt good. He moved faster and faster as he went deeper into the swamp. He felt safe—he felt at home again.

~ O ~

"Oh my God, when?" The director of the zoo had a look of dread and terror on his face as he listened intently to his assistant.

"Sometime this morning, sir, I guess. We just heard about it a short time ago."

"Where'd the plane go down?"

The young man that had brought the terrible news held a piece of paper on which he had written the information. "They say Air Caribbean Flight 568 went down just south of Alligator Alley and about thirty miles East of Naples, Florida. It was before daylight and they buried it right into the swamp."

"Oh my, oh lordy, oh dear God." The baldheaded little man held his shiny head in both hands. After a while, he looked up at his young assistant, "Have they been notified about what was being shipped on that flight?"

Rick Magers

"Yeah, Mr. Simonson insisted on it, so the men on the airboats and swamp buggies would know what to be on the lookout for."

The bald little man's hand shook as he lit a cigarette. It calmed him somewhat and he commented, "Thank Christ they listened to me when I told 'em to carry all males on one load and all females on another, just in case something like this ever happened. Those Everglades would be a great place for a King Cobra to breed if a male and female ever got together out there."

The fifteen-foot female King Cobra was being shipped to a private collection in Jamaica.

The seventeen-foot male that had escaped from a private collection in Atlanta and slithered onto a truck bound for Miami moved gracefully through the swamp toward the Florida West Coast.

He would soon find the female that escaped after the air crash. They and their offspring would make changes in the Everglades in the coming years that would last until it was finely filled in.

## The End

Perhaps?

~ *of the only Everglades on Planet Earth* ~

Rick Magers

## AFTERWORD

NOTE: Names were changed to protect the privacy of some of the characters in this book.

- A yacht returning to Key West from Andros Island on the night the terrorists departed for Paradise reported to the U. S. Coast Guard that an airplane exploded just after it flew by them.

- A third body was found when the blast area that sent Amad and Jintan to Paradise was carefully scoured by agents from Homeland Security. It was finally identified as Jerome Sennitt.

- Percy's dead body was found in a taxicab at the Tallahassee Airport. It had been stolen in Valdosta Georgia months earlier.

- Politicians are still trying to get the bounty on the pythons in the Everglades lowered, because it is affecting what they call their Fun Fun(d)

- Hussein and Rita married and have a baby boy coming soon. They are as happy as either of them had ever hoped for.

- Angelo and Christina enjoyed showing Angelina all of the places in their hometown. Their trip was made much better by the $1,000 that Burt's boss paid them for their story.

- 75-year-old Sheenie Goldberg had a stroke and died. His sister sold the house for $375,000 and went on a world cruise.

- Captain Corey McMillin took Burt and Maggie and a few of their close friends out on his father's 50' boat and performed their marriage ceremony.

- Burt's boss and best friend, Yan Shen, drove to Everglades City to go out on the boat to be Burt's Best Man. He paid for an after-ceremony party at the Camellia Street Grill, and everyone raved about the food, and enjoyed cocktails and beer while they danced to live country music by a local band.

- Abner Brown paid for the best suite at the famous Rod and Gun Club for Burt and Maggie's first night as newlyweds. The next morning they drove to Ft. Lauderdale to enjoy a ten-day cruise in the Caribbean. It was an unexpected gift from Burt's favorite uncle.

About other books by this author

- **Dark Caribbean**...is based on a true story about two offshore lobstermen battling pirates for years, and eventually begin smuggling drugs. Airplanes, airboats, 150 mph pickemup trucks, gunfire, riding alligators, wild men, wilder women—it's all in this one...and it's all true.

- **The McKannahs**...is a western adventure novel that begins in 17th century Ireland and moves to early 18th century America. Five McKannah sons and one daughter spread out across this wild new country to build their life.

- **The McKannahs ~together again~** ... the four McKannah brothers come to Montana and stand with Jesse as he confronts men intent on wiping out his Flathead Indian friends. Their sister, Aleena...well, she...

- **Carib Indian**...this is the only novel written specifically about these courageous freedom fighters. Holding wooden spears in their hand-carved canoes, they took on mighty ships full of modern soldiers that had entered the Caribbean Sea in search of slaves.

- **The Face Painter**...is a book of stories for young readers from 8 to 88.

- **The Black Widowmaker**…was a beautiful black woman who made widows of many women, but after reading her story, you might find yourself sympathizing with her.

- **Satan's Dark Angels**…is a collection of frightening stories, and now accompanies The Black Widowmaker…making two novellas in one book.

- **America**…is a book of western and other short stories.

- **A Sacred Vow**…A Memoir.

- **It's A Dog's Life**…the author's 15 year old, blind Jackrat—½ Jack Russell and ½ Rat Terrier, Dandy, who always wanted to write his autobiography. With help from Rick, he finally finished it, a short time before his death. All proceeds will go to homeless animal caregivers.

- **80 Short Stories**…is great for folks who don't like to face one long story in a novel. You'll find almost every genre in this one. Sad, funny, unbelievable, maddening, frightening, whacky, true, thought-provoking, award winning and some you will read over-and-over. (there are now 81 stories; one that I was told to never publish.) A bonus for faithful fans.

- **Ladybug and the Dragon**…is the true story of Tampa native, Katia Solomon. At two, she was diagnosed with leukemia. Rather than write a story about her, as he was asked to do by a magazine editor, Rick decided to write a small book and send the Solomon family all of the money from sales to assist them during that difficult time. Katia turned 16 in 2016 and remains in remission, but now their small house was re-possessed. It's the one her mama was raised in, and Katia loves. Rick updated the book. See pictures of Katia: **www.ladybugkatia.com**

- **The Ghosts of Chokoloskee**...a story about the ghosts of the pioneers that settled the hostile land at the edge of the Everglades—hard working folks, a psychopathic killer, a band of vigilantes, and the man they killed.

- **CALUSA ~warriors from a distant past~** This novel is about the ancient Calusa Indians. It begins in 15,000 BP in a land we now know as Siberia. A small tribe goes across the land bridge, and on into Alaska. Behind then the landbridge goes under as seas rose above it. For thousands of years, tribes branched out in search of new areas to live, where they would not be attacked by hostile tribes looking to steal women for breeding, and children to train as warriors. Many tribes went farther north, because cold and snow is what they were used to. Other tribes had learned from traders that there were unpopulated lands south, where the weather was better. Over centuries, they Calusa followed the coast in dugout canoes to San Francisco, San Diego, and on to Cabo San Lucas, where they crossed the water to Mexico, and eventually across Central America on a river, and then south along the South American coast of the Caribbean Sea. After visiting several of the islands during a long period of time, they leave Cuba and head toward Florida's west coast, where they settle in an area north of Ft. Myers. There were few people in the area they chose, so the Calusa dominated Southwest Florida for 2000 years. However, when the Spaniards arrived with germs and their cruel gene, it was the beginning of the end for the ancient Calusa.

- **2084 ~a world in peril~** This novel was not intended to be a follow up of George Orwell's novel 1984. My intent is to point out the obvious, that we humans have abused this beautiful blue planet. If we do not soon find a way to reverse our thinking, reduce the annual amount of births on an already overcrowded planet, and begin treating Planet Earth as if it is the only planet that humans will ever have to call home, then we deserve whatever punishment awaits us in the near future.

- **The Pioneers of South Florida**...Tough as nails people like Robert Roberts, who was a cattleman since the day he saw his first steer. At a very young age, Robert decided to become a cowboy, and he did—not the kind seen in the movies, where pistols shoot a hundred times. He became a legendary cowboy in the unlikely state of Florida. Upon encountering roughnecks and wannabe-tough-guys trying

Uninvited to collect money for crossing a river on free range, they found several cowboys sitting high in the saddle with a hand on their pistol. Robert and his sons and cowboys crossed rivers as they came to them.....100 or so miles south, men just as tough were taming areas thought uninhabitable from Everglades City and Chokoloskee Island to Marco Island. With no law to turn to, the locals killed the notorious killer, Edgar Watson. Tough is still required to live on Chokoloskee permanently.

**Available Christmas 2017**

## PART - II
# 2099 ~a world in repair~

I offer humble thanks to my many readers —
an author without a following of readers,
is but one more unknown writer.

Sincerely, Rick